94

34

WEAPONS AND
EQUIPMENT OF THE
SAS

SIDGWICK & JACKSON
LONDON

WEAPONS AND
EQUIPMENT OF THE
SAS

PETER
DARMAN

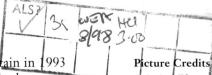

First published in Great Britain in 1993
by Sidgwick & Jackson Limited

ISBN 0 283 06141 - 3

Printed and bound in Great Britain by
BPCC Hazell Books, Aylesbury, Bucks

Sidgwick & Jackson Limited
18-21 Cavaye Place
London SW10 9PG

Editorial and Design: Brown Packaging

Quoted excerpts taken from:
Soldier 'I' SAS by Michael Paul Kennedy, published by Bloomsbury Publishing Ltd (1990)
Rogue Warrior of the SAS by Roy Bradford and Martin Dillon, published by Arrow Books Ltd (1989)
SAS: Operation Oman by Colonel Tony Jeapes, published by William Kimber & Co. Ltd (1983)
One of the Originals by Johnny Cooper, published by Pan Books Ltd (1991)
One Man's SAS by Lofty Large, published by William Kimber & Co. Ltd (1987)
The SAS by Philip Warner, published by Sphere Books Ltd (1988)
SAS: The Jungle Frontier by Peter Dickens, published by Book Club Associates (1983)
A History of the SAS Regiment by John Strawson, published by Secker & Warburg Ltd (1984)

Front cover: CRW soldier and trooper in DPM dress.
Previous pages: Observing the enemy from a camouflaged position.
Back cover: Longline's Light Strike Vehicle.

Picture Credits

Aviation Photographs International: 9 (top), 17 (top), 27, 28-29, 45, 48-49, 57 (bottom), 65 (bottom), 69 (top & bottom), 74-75, 80-81, 84-85, 87 (top), 93 (top & bottom), 102, 103, 106, 110-111, 119, 122-123, 138-139, 179 (bottom), 187 (top & bottom) **Avon Industrial Polymers Ltd:** 144, 145, 146, 148, 150 **Brown Packaging:** 6-7, 22, 23, 25 (bottom), 26, 31, 38-39, 41 (left & right), 60, 63, 95, 98-99, 135, 143 (top & bottom), 147, 149, 153 (bottom), 157 (top & bottom), 158, 160, 171 **W.J. Clow (Midlands) Ltd:** 151 **Colt Firearms:** 12, 72 **Davin Optical Ltd:** 170, 172 **Ian Hogg:** 153 (top), 156 **Ray Hutchins:** 10, 15, 36, 44, 130, 131, 134 **ITT Defense (Electro-Optical Products):** 65 (top) **Imperial War Museum:** 25 (top), 30, 51 (top), 57 (top), 108, 113 (top), 129 (top), 179 (top) **Magellan:** 90-91, 97 **Military Picture Library:** 11, 18, 47 (top) **Military Picture Library/Robin Adshead:** 43 (top), 47 (bottom), 87 (bottom), 166-167, 176-177, 185 (bottom), 191 (top) **Military Picture Library/Peter Russell:** front cover*, 2-3, 17 (bottom)*, 21, 33 (bottom)*, 35*, 66-67, 96, 125 (bottom), 140-141*, 188-189 **Military Picture Library/Tony Simpson:** 9 (bottom)* **Bob Morrison:** 126-127, 133 (top & bottom) **MREL:** 161 **Nikon UK:** 174, 175 **Photo Press:** 13, 43 (bottom), 113 (bottom), 115, 116-117, 120, 181 (bottom), 182-183, back cover **Press Association:** 162-163 **SIG Sauer:** 37 (top & bottom), 155 **Telegraph Colour Library:** 185 (top) **Thorn EMI:** 169 (top & bottom) **TRH Pictures:** 14, 33 (top), 51 (bottom), 53, 54-55, 58, 59, 61, 71, 77 (top & bottom), 79, 83 (top & bottom), 87 (bottom), 89 (top), 101 (top & bottom), 104-105, 107, 108-109, 118, 123, 125 (top), 129 (bottom), 136-137, 181 (top), 191 (bottom)

* Actors and models used in these photographs

CONTENTS

SMALL ARMS

Expert weapons skills have been instrumental in the success the SAS has experienced in its campaigns. Indeed, David Stirling, the Regiment's founder in 1941, insisted that SAS soldiers be proficient in all the small arms they were likely to meet, including foreign weapons.

For a unit that was expected to fight deep behind enemy lines, being able to use an opponent's weapons meant a patrol could fight for extended periods if need be. Since 1941, SAS soldiers have been given extensive training in the small arms of both actual and potential enemies. However, it has been the ability of individual SAS soldiers to use their small arms with great accuracy that has often been the reason for their success in battle. This fact should not be under-estimated: most soldiers in battle, because of stress, fear and fatigue, only manage to make effective use of their side arms at ranges below 100m, and the majority of shots they do fire are inaccurate. SAS soldiers use their weapons much more effectively. At Mirbat in 1972, for example, a nine-man SAS team, aided by a few local policemen and irregulars, held off an attack by 250 communist fighters. The latter's defeat on that day was due in large part to the SAS soldiers' skill in wielding assault rifles, machine guns, mortars and a 25-pounder field gun. If one were to look for the reason why SAS soldiers are so deadly in the use of small arms, it is because individual troopers try to make every shot count. The need to conserve ammunition is paramount on long-range patrols. Therefore, wild shooting is avoided and fire from machine guns is always in short, controlled bursts.

Looking through the text below, the reader will not find a wide deviation from those weapons which have been used by British soldiers since World War II, except for the use of specialist counter-terrorist weapons and those of both friendly and potentially hostile countries. However, it must always be borne in mind when talking about the SAS that it is the calibre of the individual carrying the weapon, rather than the gun itself, that makes the difference in a firefight.

Left: The SA-80 assault rifle. Because of problems with this weapon, the SAS reportedly still prefers the M16 and SLR.

Section 1
RIFLES AND ASSAULT RIFLES

Rifles and assault rifles (the latter are weapons with an automatic-fire capability) have been, and continue to be, the main personal weapon of the infantry soldier throughout the world. They are also used by special forces units, though their employment is slightly different to that seen in conventional-type engagements between two armies. The troops of the former Soviet Union, for example, were not taught to shoot at individual targets with their AK-47 assault rifles; rather, they were instructed to use them as part of a mass barrage of fire that would literally overwhelm the enemy. SAS soldiers, on the other hand, use their rifles for accurate, lethal fire at medium ranges, such as in an ambush or a conventional battle situation, where a four-man team can select and deal with individual targets at ranges of below 200m. As SAS units are invariably far from friendly re-supply or are behind enemy lines, there is a strong need to conserve ammunition. Therefore, semi-automatic or short-burst fire is usually employed. The SAS also tailors its weapons to the tactical requirement of the mission. Individual troopers would not, for example, be armed with Heckler & Koch MP5 submachine guns to conduct a desert ambush that required accurate fire up to a range of 250m. Similarly, during a hostage-rescue operation, SAS soldiers would not be equipped with rifles to storm an aircraft.

Armalite A weapon designed by the inventor Eugene Stoner while working for the Fairchild Airplane Company's Armalite Division. Designed in 1956, the production of the rifle was eventually licensed to Colt. It became known as the XM-16 and was formally adopted by the US armed forces in 1967 as the M16A1. The Armalite, designated AR-15, because of its weight and compact size, was ideally suited to jungle warfare. The weapon was used by the SAS in Borneo (1963-66) and the Regiment continues to use the M16 rifle. Its advantages over the SLR rifle are apparent: it is 150mm shorter and nearly 2kg lighter. In addition, its 5.56mm ammunition has a higher lethality at short ranges than the

7.62mm round (for specifications see the entry for the M16 assault rifle).

Belgian FN Used by the SAS during the Malayan campaign (1948-60), the FN FAL was a forerunner of the SLR and was essentialy the same weapon. However, the Belgian FN was capable of full-automatic fire as well as semi-automatic, though individual troopers often found the weapon to be hard to control and thus less accurate when fired automatically. 'Lofty' Large, an SAS veteran of its campaigns in the Far East and the Middle East, states it thus: 'The main difference between the FN and the SLR was that the FN had a three position change lever giving automatic and semi-automatic fire, whereas the SLR can only fire semi-automatic. We found the FN was too inaccurate when fired on automatic so the SLR was really just as good.' Nevertheless, the FN, like the SLR, was an extremely rugged and reliable rifle, and was suited to most types of SAS extended operations.

Type: assault rifle
Designation: FN FAL
Calibre: 7.62mm
Weight: 4.25kg (empty)
Length: 1090mm
Effective range: 650m
Rate of fire: 650-700 rounds per minute (cyclic)
Feed: 20-round box magazine
Muzzle velocity: 840 metres per second

CHINESE RIFLES

The SAS, like other special forces units that are expected to operate behind enemy lines, is familiar with the workings of the main types of Chinese rifles. These weapons are mostly based on Soviet designs, although others, in keeping with the Chinese doctrine of reverse engineering, are poor copies of Western variants. 'Cheap and nasty' is a label that can be applied to these weapons, and they are for the most part crude and poorly made.

Above right: The Chinese Type 56 assault rifle.
Below right: The M16 and M203 grenade launcher.

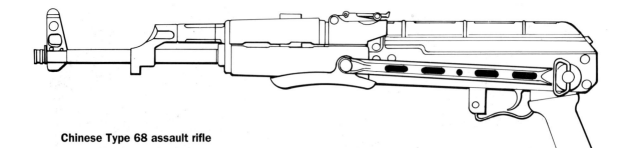

Chinese Type 68 assault rifle

Type 56 Based on the Soviet AK-47, this rifle is capable of single-shot or full-automatic fire.
Type: assault rifle
Designation: 56, 56-1 and 56-2
Calibre: 7.62mm
Weight: 3.80kg
Length: 874mm
Effective range: 300m
Rate of fire: 600 rounds per minute (cyclic)
Feed: 30-round box magazine
Muzzle velocity: 710 metres per second

Type 68 A weapon of Chinese design though the bolt-action is based on the Soviet AK-47. Capable of semi- and full-automatic fire, it is probably more accurate than the AK-47 because the barrel is longer and slightly heavier, though overall the weapon is more cumbersome.
Type: assault rifle
Calibre: 7.62mm
Weight: 3.49kg
Length: 1029mm
Effective range: 400m
Rate of fire: 750 rounds per minute (cyclic)
Feed: 15- and 30-round box magazine
Muzzle velocity: 730 metres per second

Colt Commando The most compact and smallest version of the M16A2 rifle. In a combat situation the Commando can be brought to bear on a target very quickly. Its small size makes it ideal for counter-terrorist operations, and it has been used in such a role by the SAS in Northern Ireland.
Type: assault rifle
Designation: Model 733 Commando
Calibre: 5.56mm
Weight: 2.44kg (empty)

Length: 760mm (butt extended); 680mm (butt telescoped)
Effective range: 400m
Rate of fire: 700-1000 rounds per minute (cyclic)
Feed: 20- or 30-round box magazine
Muzzle velocity: 829 metres per second

Heckler & Koch G3 The standard-issue rifle of the German Army for the past 30 years, the G3 has been seen in the hands of SAS troopers on numerous occasions, especially in Northern Ireland. As with most things manufactured in the Federal Republic of Germany, the G3 is well engineered and extremely robust and reliable. Its ability to perform well under adverse weather conditions has endeared it not only to the SAS, but also to the US SEALs and Rangers.
Type: assault rifle
Calibre: 7.62mm
Weight: 4.4kg (empty)
Length: 1025mm
Effective range: 400m
Rate of fire: 500-600 rounds per minute (cyclic)
Feed: 20-round box magazine
Muzzle velocity: 780-800 metres per second

Heckler & Koch G8 This rifle has an automatic and three-round burst facility, as well as being able to fire in the semi-automatic mode. It can also be converted to belt or magazine feed and has a heavy, quick-change barrel and telescopic sight as standard. The rifle was designed for counter-insurgency work and is used by the German counter-terrorist unit, GSG 9. It is also undoubtedly used by the SAS in Ulster.
Type: assault rifle optimized for counter-terrorist work
Calibre: 7.62mm

Above: The M16 assault rifle has been in SAS use since the mid-1960s, when it was used in Borneo.

Weight: 8.15kg (empty, with bipod)
Length: 1030mm
Effective range: 800m
Rate of fire: 800 rounds per minute (cyclic)
Feed: 20- or 50-round magazine
Muzzle velocity: 800 metres per second

Heckler & Koch G41 Essentially a G3 developed to fire 5.56mm ammunition, the G41 has several attributes, in addition to it firing the lighter, more lethal 5.56mm round, that makes it attractive to units such as the SAS: low noise, dustproof cover for cartridge case ejection port, three-round burst capability and ability to fit a 30-round magazine. The G41 is equipped with a fixed butt or a retractable one as required.

Type: assault rifle
Calibre: 5.56mm
Weight: 4.1kg (fixed butt, empty);
4.35kg (retracting butt, empty)
Length: 997mm (fixed butt); 806mm (butt retracted)
Effective range: 400m
Rate of fire: 850 rounds per minute
Feed: 30-round box magazine
Muzzle velocity: 800 metres per second

Lee-Enfield .303-inch One of the finest military bolt-action rifles ever made, the Rifle, Short, Magazine, Lee-Enfield was used by the Special Air Service in World War II, particularly in the North African desert. The SAS, like most

World War II special forces units, were mostly quite satisfied with standard-issue weapons, though the opportunity to acquire a German MP40 submachine gun, for example, was never passed over. Though the Lee-Enfield's rate of fire – being bolt-operated – could be slow, it was an extremely reliable weapon and one that held twice as many rounds as enemy models. The rifle was also used by members of the Long Range Desert Group.

Type: bolt-action rifle
Designation: Rifle, Short, Magazine, Lee-Enfield
Calibre: .303-inch
Weight: 4.13kg
Length: 1132mm
Effective range: 800m
Feed: 10-round detachable box magazine
Muzzle velocity: 670 metres per second

M1 Carbine A weapon that was produced in large numbers in World War II, the M1 Carbine was ideally suited to the subsequent jungle operations the SAS conducted in Malaya between 1948 and 1960. It was lightweight and had an excellent rate of fire, as well as being reliable and easy to clean and maintain. As such it was carried by many of the Regiment's troopers during the Malayan campaign.

Above: The Colt Commando, a shortened version of the M16. Used by the SAS in Northern Ireland.

However, it did have drawbacks: its accuracy was poor beyond 100m and, more importantly, the round the M1 used had a low lethality. This was because the gun fired what was virtually a pistol bullet which had poor ballistic shape for long flight. Its rapid fall-off in velocity combined with the low muzzle velocity to result in a low striking energy. It has been asserted that wearing a leather jerkin and overcoat was defence against a Carbine ball at 50m! Nevertheless, for the 1950s the M1 was a useful weapon for low-intensity work at short ranges. It is unlikely that the SAS used it after the Malayan campaign ended in 1960.

Type: semi-automatic rifle
Calibre: 0.3-inch
Weight: 2.48kg (unloaded)
Length: 905mm
Effective range: 300m
Feed: 15- or 30-round detachable box magazine
Muzzle velocity: 593 metres per second

M16 The result of the US Army's desire for a small gun that could fire a lighter cartridge, the M16 has become one of the most successful assault rifles in the world. The M16 weighed less than its predecessors, the M1 and M14 rifles, thus allowing individual soldiers to carry more of the lighter 5.56mm ammunition. The SAS was quick to adopt the M16 for its operations, notable examples of its use being in Borneo (1963-66), Oman (1970-76) and during the 1982

Falklands War. In Borneo the SAS, and British troops in general, found the US 5.56mm M193 bullet to be ineffective beyond a range of 400m. In addition, the bullet tended to be easily deflected by branches and other obstacles that occur in the jungle. Therefore, the heavier, slower moving European SS109 bullet was preferred.

The M16 is excellent for jungle warfare, being short, light and having a high lethality at short ranges – all qualities which endear it to fighting in a terrain which is characterised by poor visibility. In the desert the rifle performs less well: it does not stand up particularly well to the sandy conditions and its long-range accuracy is not particularly good. Despite this, the SAS used the M16 in both Aden (1964-67) and Oman (1970-76) and found it gave reasonable service. The rifle is generally lighter and uses lightweight ammunition compared to the SLR, for example, which is always a godsend to troops who have to carry their weapons and ammunition on foot over long distances. It also has low recoil, making it comfortable to fire.

The M16 does require frequent (daily) and thorough cleaning (it was originally sold as a self-cleaning gun), though this is not a particular problem for SAS soldiers, who are taught to care meticulously for their weapons when on active duty. A rather more serious problem with the rifle is its inability to withstand rough handling, a grave matter for troops who often find them-selves deep behind enemy lines and put heavy demands upon both themselves and the equipment they use.

Above: A stack of M16s. Originally sold as a self-cleaning gun, the model in fact requires daily maintenance to prevent fouling in the gas passages.

The current model of the M16 is the M16A2. The US, and SAS, version is capable or three-round bursts as well as single-shot fire but does not have a full-automatic facility, whereas the Canadian model has the full-automatic option plus single-shot but no three-round burst setting (the latter was designed to conserve ammunition on the battlefield and deter wild firing). It is anticipated that the M16 will remain in SAS use until well into the next century.

Type: assault rifle
Designation: M16A2
Calibre: 5.56mm
Weight: 3.40kg (empty)
Length: 1000mm
Effective range: 400m
Rate of fire: 700-900 rounds per minute (cyclic)
Feed: 20- or 30-round box magazine
Muzzle velocity: 991 metres per second (M193 bullet); 948 metres per second (SS109 bullet)

Ruger Mini-14 Essentially a scaled down version of the M1 Garand, the Mini-14, introduced by Sturm, Ruger & Co. in 1973, has a lower recoil force than the M1 because it fires the 5.56mm bullet. This means that a reasonable degree of accuracy can be maintained with the rifle, even when firing at full-automatic – which makes it an attractive weapon to specialist units such as the SAS for counter-terrorist operations. The Mini-14 is also used by US Special Weapons and Tactics (SWAT) teams.

The following specifications are for the AC-556 selective fire version of the Mini-14. The rifle, which is specially designed for law-enforcement and military use, has three fire control settings: semi-automatic, full-automatic, or three-round burst.

Type: assault rifle
Designation: AC-556
Calibre: 5.56mm
Weight: 2.89kg
Length: 984mm
Effective range: 300m
Rate of fire: 750 rounds per minute (cyclic)
Feed: 5-, 20- or 30-round box magazine
Muzzle velocity: 1058 metres per second

SA-80 The new standard-issue infantry weapon of the British Army and a replacement for the SLR, the SA-80 is capable of semi- and full-automatic fire. First deliveries were made to the Army in the summer of 1984. The rifle suffered teething troubles – magazines falling off, fore-ends breaking, to name but two – which have not yet been solved. This is a pity because the rifle is light, easy to handle, has low recoil, excellent sights and is accurate up to a range of 300m.

Will the SAS like the SA-80? It is difficult to ascertain, although the rifle is handier to use and carry than the M16, for example. Factors that will endear it to the Regiment are its accuracy and range, though until its many problems are sorted out it will stick to tried and tested models.

Type: assault rifle
Designation: L85A1
Calibre: 5.56mm
Weight: 3.8kg (without sight and magazine)
Length: 785mm
Effective range: 300m
Rate of fire: 650-800 rounds per minute (cyclic)

Above: In SAS service since the mid-1950s, the SLR has excellent long-range accuracy.

Feed: 30-round box magazine
Muzzle velocity: 940 metres per second

SLR The Self-Loading Rifle was the standard individual weapon of the British Army from the mid-1950s to the mid-1980s. Adapted from the Belgian *Fusil Automatique Légèr* (FAL), the SLR is reliable, robust and can operate effectively under adverse weather conditions, though unlike its Belgian counterpart, it cannot fire at full-automatic, only semi-automatic. Its attributes made the rifle attractive to units such as the SAS, and the gun saw service with the Regiment in Borneo, Oman and the Falklands.

Pictures of SAS troopers in Borneo nearly always include the SLR. This is rather surprising for the rifle was not particularly suited to jungle warfare, being long and cumbersome with a powerful cartridge and bullet designed for long-range firing. However, it must be remembered that at the time the Regiment did not have a lot of choice as the there were never enough M16s to go around and there were no other rifles available. Nevertheless, the ferocity of the SLR's round cannot be doubted, as Mike Wilkes, an officer with A Squadron during the Borneo campaign, relates: 'when a heavy SLR bullet goes through a tree it doesn't make a clean hole but shatters the wood into tiny fibres as though it

were explosive, and the top of a two-inch sapling is wrenched off leaving a stump like a shaving-brush. Imagine one going into you. Salutary.'

The SLR really came into its own in the desert, where accurate long-range fire is called for. Captain Ian Cheshire, an SAS troop commander in Oman, relates an interesting story concerning the SLR and the *firqat* troops he was training: 'They still don't really like them. Many of them are small men as you know, and the FN is too heavy for them. They keep harping on about the Kalashnikov, so we got hold of one and made them fire it at a hundred yards automatic; them we made them shoot an FN semi-automatic and compared the hits. They're good shots and most had all twenty shots on target with the FN but they'd be lucky to get more than five with the Kalashnikov, so I think we've probably cured them of wanting to fire fully automatic the whole time.' It is believed that the SAS was among the first units to be issued with SA-80s, though the problems with the latter means SLRs are still in use with the Regiment.

Type: assault rifle
Designation: L1A1
Calibre: 7.62mm
Weight: 4.30kg
Length: 1143mm
Effective range: 600m (with SUIT – Sight Unit Infantry Trilux – fitted)
Feed: 20-round-box magazine
Muzzle velocity: 838 metres per second

SOVIET RIFLES

The SAS is extremely familiar with the weapons issued to the troops of the Soviet Union (or the Commonwealth of Independent States as the area is now known). The weapons were, from the outset, designed for ease of maintenance and cleaning, to be soldier-proof, simple and robust. Around 50 million AK-47s have been produced, testimony in itself to the success of the design. SAS troops are regularly trained in the use of Soviet weapons, particularly the AK series.

AK-47 Capable of semi- and full-automatic fire, the AK-47, because of its distinctive curved magazine, is one of the most easily recognised rifles currently in use. This simple, robust weapon has been seen in the hands of terrorists and guerrilla fighters throughout the world. Its main faults are its poor accuracy beyond 300m and the noise of its safety/fire selector lever which makes clandestine work difficult.

Type: assault rifle
Calibre: 7.62mm
Weight: 4.30kg
Length: 699mm (butt folded); 869mm (extended)
Effective range: 300m
Rate of fire: 600 rounds per minute (cyclic)
Feed: 30-round box magazine
Muzzle velocity: 710 metres per second

AKM A modernised version of the AK-47 but a weapon which does not differ fundamentally from the operation of its predecessor. The AKM has a wooden stock while the folding stock version is designated AKMS. With regard to performance and handling, the AKM is no different to the AK-47.

Type: assault rifle
Calibre: 7.62mm
Length: 876mm
Effective range: 300m
Rate of fire: 600 rounds per minute (cyclic)
Feed: 30-round box magazine
Muzzle velocity: 715 metres per second

AK-74 A smaller calibre version of the AKM. The AK-74 has an effective muzzle brake that allows burst fire without the muzzle moving away from the line-of-sight. This, together with the better shape of the smaller bullet and the lower recoil, makes it more accurate than the AKM.

Type: assault rifle
Calibre: 5.45mm

Weight: 3.6kg (unloaded)
Length: 930mm
Effective range: 400m
Rate of fire: 650 rounds p ..inute
Feed: 30-round plastic box magazine
Muzzle velocity: 900 metres per second

Steyr AUG This futuristic-looking bullpup assault rifle has been occasionally used by the SAS, mainly for counter-terrorist duties in Northern Ireland. It is capable of semi- and full-automatic fire or, instead of the full-automatic option, a three-round burst capability. The AUG is one of the best 5.56mm rifles currently in production, having excellent accuracy, optical sights, reliability and, essential for special forces operations, can take a lot of punishment (in one test a six-ton truck was driven over an AUG 15 times before anything snapped, and even then the rifle was still able to shoot – this compares most favourably with rifles such as the M16 and SA-80, for example). In addition, the weapon can be turned into anything from a submachine gun to a light support weapon by simply swapping parts. All in all, the AUG points the way forward with regard to future rifle design.

Type: assault rifle
Designation: Steyr *Armee-Universal-Gewehr*
Calibre: 5.56mm
Weight: 3.60kg (empty)
Length: 790mm
Effective range: 500m
Rate of fire: 650 rounds per minute (cyclic)
Feed: 30- and 42-round clear plastic magazine (the firer can see how many rounds are left)
Muzzle velocity: 970 metres per second

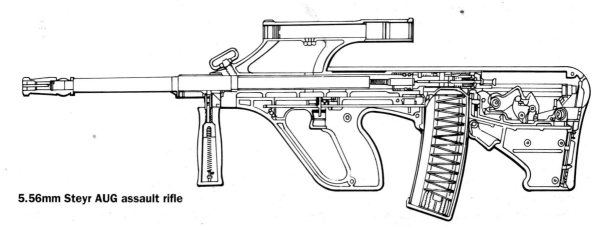

5.56mm Steyr AUG assault rifle

SUBMACHINE GUNS

A submachine gun is a weapon of pistol calibre which has an automatic or selective-fire capability, is magazine fed and can be fired from the shoulder or hip. Submachine guns are normally used for close-range combat. The SAS has always used submachine guns, though their specific employment has changed over the years. During World War II, SAS units carried submachine guns on raids, using them alongside rifles and pistols. Pictures of SAS troops taken after they had captured the Italian port of Termoli in October 1943, for example, show individual soldiers carrying a captured German submachine gun, a Thompson submachine gun, as well as a British Lee-Enfield rifle.

As the bolt-action rifle gave way to the semi-automatic variety in the years following the end of World War II, SAS soldiers dropped the submachine gun, preferring the semi-automatic rifle which had the ability to lay down a barrage of sustained, accurate fire but which did not waste valuable ammunition. The era of the submachine gun appeared to have ended. However, the rise in international terrorism and hostage-taking which occurred in western Europe in the 1960s prompted many governments to establish dedicated anti-terrorist units. In Britain the SAS was detailed to assume a counter-terrorist role which also covered the quasi-military war which had began in Northern Ireland in 1969.

Suddenly the Regiment was training to storm buildings, trains and aircraft to free hostages from armed terrorists, and to lay ambushes and stalk terrorists in the countryside and towns of Northern Ireland. The SAS needed a weapon which fulfilled the perceived tactical need for a short-range, high-volume-of-fire weapon which was compact and could be brought to bear quickly on the target (who was often moving and was in poor light). The submachine gun was back in business.

In the MP5 range of submachine guns produced by Heckler & Koch the SAS has a weapon which fulfils all of these criteria. It must be borne in mind that these weapons are totally unsuitable for operations in the field. Their high rate of fire – 800-1000 rounds per minute is not unusual – means a magazine can be emptied very quickly, and small-sized, long-range patrols do not have an inexhaustible supply of ammunition. In addition, they tend to be inaccurate when compared to rifles (most submachine guns fire from an open bolt, i.e. when the gun is cocked the bolt is kept to the rear; when the trigger is pressed the bolt flies violently forward several centimetres and is then stopped abruptly, resulting in a sudden shift in weight which disrupts the general aim).

Despite its shortcomings for field work, the submachine gun is ideally suited to counter-terrorist/hostage-rescue work, where the action is invariably over in seconds but in that time the unit needs to lay down a large amount of fire to disable individual terrorists (this normally means keeping the latters' hands away from any concealed weapons or explosives they may be carrying, or hitting them with a volley of shots before they can bring their weapons to bear). Therefore, it can be stated with some certainty that the SAS will continue to use submachine guns well into the next century.

CHINESE SUBMACHINE GUNS

It is extremely unlikely that the SAS would have any contact with Chinese models; indeed, they would probably wish to avoid them like the plague given their general poor engineering and limited lethality. Nevertheless, in line with the Regiment's claim that its soldiers can go anywhere and use the enemy's weapons, an example is given of the type of submachine gun currently in service in China.

Type 64 A silenced weapon which is extremely cumbersome and ill-balanced. It fires the Soviet 7.62mm pistol cartridge but is a poor gun compared to the models on offer in the West.

Above right: An early Chinese submachine gun.
Below right: The Ingram is compact and lethal, but too clumsy for hostage-rescue operations.

Type: silenced submachine gun
Designation: Type 64
Calibre: 7.62mm
Weight: 3.40kg (empty)
Length: 843mm (stock open); 635mm (stock closed)
Effective range: 135m
Rate of fire: 1315 rounds per minute (cyclic)
Feed: 30-round curved box magazine
Muzzle velocity: 513 metres per second

Ingram submachine gun The Ingram was the SAS's primary weapon for Counter Revolutionary Warfare (CRW) operations until 1980, when it was replaced by the Heckler & Koch MP5 submachine gun. In 1977 terrorists had hijacked a Lufthansa Boeing 737 airliner and flew it to Mogadishu, Somalia. The aircraft was subsequently stormed by the German counterterrorist squad, GSG 9, and all the passengers were freed. Two SAS soldiers had assisted in the operation: Sergeant Barry Davies and Major Alistair Morrison. The performance of the MP5 at Mogadishu, particularly in the confined space of an aircraft cabin, convinced the Regiment that the German weapon was more suitable for hostage-rescue operations than the Ingram, and so the decision was taken to adopt it.

The decision was a good one. The Ingram is in fact nothing exceptional as a submachine gun, being rather clumsy and, much worse for CRW operations, inaccurate, especially when fired one-handed. Its only good points are its compactness and the ability to attach a silencer. However, the SAS still appears to favour it for work in Northern Ireland, probably because of its high rate of fire and small size.

Type: submachine gun
Designation: Model 10
Calibre: 9mm
Weight: 3.46kg (including 32-round magazine)
Length: 269mm (stock telescoped); 548mm (stock extended)
Effective range: 40m
Rate of fire: 1090 rounds per minute
Feed: 32-round magazine
Muzzle velocity: 366 metres per second

Heckler & Koch HK 53 Classed as a submachine gun although it fires 5.56mm ammunition. Based on the MP5, though having larger dimensions, this weapon has found great favour with the SAS in Northern Ireland, probably because it can be used either as a submachine gun or an assault rifle.

Type: submachine gun
Calibre: 5.56mm
Weight: 3.05kg (empty)
Length: 755mm (butt extended); 563mm (butt retracted)
Effective range: 250m
Rate of fire: 700 rounds per minute (cyclic)
Feed: 25-round box magazine
Muzzle velocity: 750 metres per second

Heckler & Koch MP5 Along with the Browning High Power handgun, the MP5 submachine gun is the weapon most associated with the SAS. The weapon was put to devastating use in 1980 during the siege of the Iranian Embassy. On 5 May 1980, members of 'Pagoda' Troop, dressed in black assault suits and carrying MP5s, stormed the building to free over 20 hostages being held captive by six terrorists of the Democratic Revolutionary Front for the Liberation of Arabistan. The SAS blew in the windows of the Embassy at the front and rear and then swept inside. The soldiers cleared the building with their side arms, eventually killing five of the terrorists. One of those involved was Soldier 'I', the SAS sergeant whose memoirs were published under that name. He was carrying a Heckler & Koch during the rescue and describes its use as he helped clear the building: 'I jabbed my MP5 into the fire position and let off a burst of twenty rounds.' The success of Operation 'Nimrod' was due in large part to the effectiveness of the MP5.

Why is the weapon so suited to hostage-rescue operations? The most important aspect of the MP5 is that it fires from a closed bolt. Most submachine guns fire from an open bolt which means that the bolt flies forward to chamber a round and then fires it when the trigger is pulled. This results in a shift in the gun's balance,

Left: The MP5 possesses all the attributes needed for hostage-rescue work: compactness, reliability, accuracy, and devastating firepower.

resulting in the shot often being off target. However, the MP5 starts with the bolt closed; all that happens when the trigger is pulled is that the hammer is released which fires the cartridge. Thus there is no shift in balance and the shot goes where it is aimed. This is the principal reason it is chosen for hostage-rescue work – it must be borne in mind that when a squad enters a room full of terrorists and hostages, the action is usually over in under four seconds – where the first shot must always count. In addition, and this too must not be underestimated, the MP5 is an extremely reliable weapon – it rarely jams.

As well as having excellent open sights, the MP5 can be fitted with image intensifiers, optical sights, aiming projectors and infrared sights. All variants offer a choice of single-shot, full-automatic or three-round burst fire. The SAS is expected to use the MP5 well into the next century; quite simply, there is no submachine gun in existence or under development that can beat it for performance and reliability.

MP5A2 and A3 These versions differ only in the fact that the A3 has a single metal strut stock which can be slid forward to reduce the overall length of the weapon, whereas the A2 has a fixed butt stock.

Type: submachine gun
Calibre: 9mm
Weight: 2.55kg (empty)
Length: 680mm (fixed butt); 660mm (butt extended); 490mm (butt retracted)
Effective range: 200m
Rate of fire: 800 rounds per minute (cyclic)
Feed: 15- or 30-round box magazine
Muzzle velocity: 400 metres per second

MP5SD The silenced version of the MP5. The gun is designed so that the bullet leaves the muzzle at subsonic velocity, thus preventing a sonic shock wave in flight.

Type: silenced submachine gun
Calibre: 9mm
Weight: 2.90kg (empty)
Length: 550mm
Effective range: 200m
Rate of fire: 800 rounds per minute (cyclic)
Feed: 15- or 30-round curved magazine
Muzzle velocity: 285 metres per second

MP5K A weapon specifically designed for special police and counter-terrorist work, being shortened to facilitate concealment in clothing or any other confined space.

The weapon has been used on occasion by the SAS in Northern Ireland. The following is taken from the statement of an SAS soldier during a contact with IRA terrorists which resulted in the deaths of two Republican gunmen, Daniel Doherty and William Fleming, on 6 December 1984: 'I was firing automatic with my MP5K submachine gun. I fired a burst. The motor-cycle kept on accelerating towards me and I was forced to jump to my left to avoid being run down. I kept on firing as the motor-cyclist was adjacent to me and just slightly past me. I couldn't be sure if I was striking him or not...During the engagement I fired a total of 30 rounds from my magazine.'

Type: submachine gun
Calibre: 9mm
Weight: 2kg (empty)
Length: 325mm
Effective range: 200m
Rate of fire: 900 rounds per minute (cyclic)
Feed: 15- or 30-round box magazine
Muzzle velocity: 375 metres per second

Heckler & Koch MP5/10 This gun is similar to the MP5 except that it is chambered for the 10mm Auto cartridge which is used by the FBI. The gun, when used with hollow point bullets, has more stopping power than the MP5.

MP40 This is the famous German submachine gun of World War II which is erroneously called the Schmeisser. SAS soldiers, along with most other Allied troops, counted themselves lucky if they could lay their hands on one of these weapons. The MP40 was robust, simple, reliable, compact, easy to maintain and clean, and could fire almost any type of 9mm ammunition. MP40s were still being used by SAS troops as late as 1963, when members of the Regiment conducted clandestine mission into Yemen.

Type: submachine gun
Calibre: 9mm
Weight: 4.70kg
Length: 630mm (stock folded)
Effective range: 150m

Rate of fire: 500 rounds per minute (cyclic)
Feed 32-round box magazine
Muzzle velocity: 365 metres per second

Owen submachine gun A weapon that was used by the SAS during its campaign in Malaya (1948-60). An Australian weapon, the Owen's magazine points vertically upwards from the body. The SAS used the weapon because it could be easily obtained from the Australians. It was also ideally suited to jungle warfare, being extremely reliable and very accurate. Though the Owen was rather heavy and was not easy to strip, its good points outweighed the bad and it proved effective in action.

Type: submachine gun
Calibre: 9mm
Weight: 4.815kg
Length: 813mm
Effective range: 150m
Rate of fire: 700 rounds per minute (cyclic)
Feed: 33-round vertical box magazine
Muzzle velocity: 420 metres per second

SOVIET SUBMACHINE GUNS

Soviet submachine guns are noted for their overall robustness. The PPSh-41 of World War II, for example, functioned almost without any maintenance. This made them extremely attractive weapons to soldiers fighting in adverse conditions. They are also simple to use, another factor that endears them to troops. Though it is unlikely that the SAS would have any use for Soviet submachine guns, troopers from the Regiment receive instruction in their use as part of the familiarisation training in foreign weapons.

AKSU-74 A 5.45mm calibre weapon which suffers from problems with muzzle blast and flash due to it using a rifle cartridge in a short barrel. Its internal mechanism is basically that of the AK-74 rifle and it is very reliable and robust.

Calibre: 5.45mm
Weight: not known
Length: 420mm (butt folded); 675mm (butt extended)
Effective range: not known
Rate of fire: 800 rounds per minute (cyclic)
Feed: 30-round magazine
Muzzle velocity: 800 metres per second

PPSh-41 This is included because it was produced in such vast quantities during World War II that almost every nation that came under Soviet influence after the war was equipped with it. As such, SAS soldiers would have received training in its use – although this would not have required much as the gun was designed with simplicity in mind. The PPSh was incredibly tough and reliable, performing well even in the harsh conditions of the Russian winter. Though long obsolete, the gun is still in use in some parts of the world.

Calibre: 7.62mm
Weight: 5.40kg
Length: 828mm
Effective range: 100m
Rate of fire: 900 round per minute (cyclic)
Feed: 71-round drum or 35-round box magazine
Muzzle velocity: 800 metres per second

Above: The Sterling is one of the most reliable submachine guns currently in service. The silenced version is used by the SAS in Ulster.

Sten gun A weapon widely used by the SAS in World War II, particularly in the weeks and months after the D-Day landings of June 1944, when SAS parties were parachuted behind enemy lines to liaise with and organise Resistance groups (which were armed with large quantities of Stens). The Sten was an effective weapon and one that worked well in adverse weather conditions such as extreme heat and in very cold conditions. It was also very easy to strip and maintain.

However, it did have its drawbacks: the magazine was always a source of stoppages and it was not particularly accurate. Nevertheless, if it was looked after the Sten was virtually

indestructible. Despite its shortcomings, the Sten remained in service with the British Army until the mid-1950s, being replaced by the Sterling.

The following information is for the Mark II version of the weapon.

Calibre: 9mm
Weight: 3.70kg
Length: 762mm
Effective range: 160m
Rate of fire: 550 rounds per minute (cyclic)
Feed: 32-round box magazine
Muzzle velocity: 365 metres per second

Sterling In service with the British Army since 1956, the Sterling is a robust, reliable and simple weapon that is still used by the SAS in Northern

Above: Royal Marines in Catania, Sicily, August 1943. The Thompson, such as the one carried by the leading soldier, was also used by the SAS.

Ireland. The Regiment favours the silenced version which differs from the standard model in that the barrel is shorter and perforated to bleed off the propellant gases to reduce muzzle velocity to subsonic speed. In addition, the barrel is encased inside a sound suppressor, making the whole weapon longer and more cumbersome than the standard model.

Standard Sterling (Mk 4)
Designation: L2A3
Calibre: 9mm
Weight: 2.72kg (empty)

Length: 690mm (butt extended); 483mm (butt retracted)
Effective range: 200m
Rate of fire: 550 rounds per minute (cyclic)
Feed: 34-round magazine
Muzzle velocity: 390 metres per second

Silenced Sterling (Mk 5)
Designation: L34A1
Calibre: 9mm
Weight: 3.60kg (empty)
Length: 864mm (butt extended); 660mm (butt retracted)
Effective range: 150m
Rate of fire: 565 rounds per minute (cyclic)
Feed: 34-round magazine
Muzzle velocity: 310 metres per second

Thompson The famous 'Tommy Gun' of World War II. The Thompson submachine gun was used by the SAS throughout the war, accompanying soldiers on hit-and-run raids behind enemy lines in North Africa, operations in Sicily and Italy, and in northwest Europe (1944-45). It was an extremely accurate and reliable weapon, though rather weighty. In addition, if the drum magazine was used the bullets had a habit of sliding back and forth and rattling inside the casing, making the gun rather unsuitable for clandestine night-time work. Despite this, SAS troops and Commandos preferred the Thompson to other submachine guns on offer.

The following information relates to the M1 which had a box magazine, as opposed to the M1928 version which had a 50-round drum magazine.
Designation: M1
Calibre: 11.43mm
Weight: 4.74kg
Length: 813mm
Effective range: 150m
Rate of fire: 700 rounds per minute (cyclic)
Feed: 20- or 30-round box magazine
Muzzle velocity: 280 metres per second

Uzi This famous Israeli weapon has been used by many police and special forces units throughout the world. It is probable that the SAS acquired several when the gun was produced

Above: An Israeli soldier armed with an Uzi submachine gun edges forward during the battle for Jerusalem in the Six-Day War of 1967.

under licence by the Belgian firm *Fabrique Nationale*. The Uzi is reliable, compact and very easy to use in the dark because of the positioning of the magazine in the pistol-grip. It is also a very robust weapon.
Calibre: 9mm
Weight: 3.70kg (empty)
Length: 650mm (butt extended); 470mm (butt retracted)
Effective range: 150m
Rate of fire: 600 rounds per minute (cyclic)
Feed: 25- and 32-round magazine
Muzzle velocity: 400 metres per second

Section 3
MACHINE GUNS

On 19 July 1972, a nine-man SAS team, together with 25 Gendarmes and 20 *askar* tribesmen, based at the Dhofari town of Mirbat, fought off an attack by 250 enemy guerrillas armed with Kalashnikov automatic rifles and backed up by anti-tank weapons. This incredible feat owed a lot to both the training and coolness of the individual SAS soldiers, and also their possession of a Browning 0.5-inch heavy machine gun and a 7.62mm General Purpose Machine Gun (GPMG), as well as an 81mm mortar and a 25-pounder field gun. The machine guns were situated on the roof of a building called the 'Batt House', and from this position throughout the battle they kept up an accurate, sustained fire against the enemy. At the end of the battle, 30 dead guerrillas were left behind, though many more had been wounded. Undoubtedly the machine guns had played a major part in securing victory for the SAS.

In fact, machine guns have played an integral part in SAS operations since the Regiment's creation in 1941. Why? The machine gun is first and foremost a fire-support weapon: the light machine gun forms the support element for the rifle squad and covers the riflemen as they advance. The GPMG forms the support for the battalion, laying down fire across specific areas to inhibit enemy movement. For a four-man SAS patrol the advantages of having machine-gun support are obvious: fire support for tactical manoeuvres and destructive firepower for raiding parties. In addition, they can be used for air defence if need be.

The main disadvantage for an SAS patrol on foot equipped with a machine gun is the large amount of ammunition needed. Though this is usually distributed among patrol members, the load each man can end up carrying can be prohibitive. For example, it is not unusual for 1000 rounds of GPMG ammunition to be distributed between the patrol, in addition to personal weapons and equipment.

Ameli A Spanish belt-fed weapon which resembles the German MG42 on a smaller scale

and uses a similar mechanism to the G3 rifle. The SAS purchased a number in 1989, when the Regiment was looking for a belt-fed 5.56mm machine gun.

Calibre: 5.56mm
Weight: 5.20kg
Length: 970mm
Effective range: 1000m
Rate of fire: 900 rounds per minute (cyclic)
Feed: belt or 100- or 200-round box magazine
Muzzle velocity: 875 metres per second

Bren gun Probably the finest light machine gun of all time. Robust, reliable, accurate and simple to use, the Bren gun took part in many SAS actions during World War II and afterwards, especially in Oman and the Radfan. There are so many examples of its use but one will suffice to illustrate its effectiveness. In July 1944, in eastern France, A Squadron, 1 SAS, was conducting an operation against enemy forces codenamed 'Houndsworth'. The SAS had established a base and were training the *Maquis* (French Resistance) to use Brens. The Germans had moved troops into the area, including Russian ex-prisoners of war officered by Germans, and were taking hostages and burning property. They captured some *Maquis* sympathisers in the village of Montsauche and decided to move them by road to their garrison headquarters.

The SAS and *Maquis* organised an ambush to free the hostages. The Brens were set up to establish killing grounds. When the convoy came into sight the front vehicle was stopped with explosives, and thereafter it was a massacre as the enemy troops tried to leave their trucks but were mown down by the Brens. The operation was a stunning success and all the hostages were released. The Brens, which had been handled by inexperienced men, had performed impeccably.

Twenty years later, Lieutenant-Colonel Johnny Cooper, an SAS veteran, was teaching

Above right: A Bren gun in action in World War II.
Below right: The modern version of the Bren, the Light Machine Gun which fires the 7.62mm round.

Above: The 0.5-inch Browning machine gun, a weapon often mounted on World War II SAS jeeps. It is still in service with armies around the world.

Yemeni royalist guerrillas to use the Bren against their communist, Egyptian-backed enemies: 'We'd already started training the Yemenis with the weapons we'd brought in, especially the Bren gun which is one of the most simplest weapons to train the guerrilla on. We organised the men into little sections of between five and seven men each – gun sections or killing groups. Because of the language difficulties (the Yemeni hill dialects are extremely difficult even with a good knowledge of Arabic), we didn't go into tactics at all. We just showed them how to get down behind the gun, how to make the best use of cover, how long to fire your burst and how not to overheat your weapon.'

The Bren is still in service, although it is known as the L4 and chambers the 7.62mm NATO round.

Designation: L4A4
Calibre: 7.62mm
Weight: 8.68kg
Length: 1156mm
Effective range: 600m
Rate of fire: 520 rounds per minute (cyclic)
Feed: 30-round box magazine
Muzzle velocity: 838 metres per second

Browning M1919A4 The machine gun which was often mounted on World War II SAS jeeps. As such it was a reliable, accurate and easy to maintain weapon, ideally suited to shooting up parked Axis aircraft on a North African airfield.

Calibre: 0.3-inch
Weight: 14.06kg
Length: 1044mm
Effective range: 1500m
Rate of fire: 400-500 rounds per minute (cyclic)
Feed: belt
Muzzle velocity: 860 metres per second

Browning 0.5-inch Again, a machine gun which found its way onto SAS jeeps during World War II, as well as being mounted on Long Range Desert Group vehicles. Like the M1919, this weapon was reliable, accurate and capable of sustained fire using a heavy barrel. It was also a fearsome man-stopper and was also, when using armour-piercing rounds, capable of defeating light armour.

Designation: M2HB
Calibre: 0.5-inch
Weight: 38.1kg
Length: 1654mm
Effective range: 1800m
Rate of fire: 450-575 rounds per minute (cyclic)
Feed: belt
Muzzle velocity: 884 metres per second

CHINESE MACHINE GUNS

Surprisingly, Chinese machine guns are rather better than one would expect, though the fact that they are again largely based on Soviet models, and that the Soviets were generally manufacturers of good machine guns, may explain why.

Type 56 A gas-operated, belt-fed weapon that can function in the general purpose role. It fires an obsolete 7.62mm cartridge which gives it good range and penetration.
Calibre: 7.62mm
Weight: 7.10kg (empty)
Length: 1036mm
Effective range: 800m
Rate of fire: 700 rounds per minute (cyclic)
Feed: 100-round continuous metal belt
Muzzle velocity: 700 metres per second

Type 74 Little is known of this gas-operated weapon, though it is thought to employ a modified Kalashnikov mechanism.

Calibre: 7.62mm
Weight: 6.20kg
Length: 1070mm
Effective range: 600m
Rate of fire: 150 rounds per minute (cyclic)
Feed: 101-round drum magazine
Muzzle velocity: 735 metres per second

GPMG The General Purpose Machine Gun is one of the most famous weapons ever used by the SAS and one that has accompanied the Regiment in every one of its campaigns since it was introduced into service in 1957. It is reliable, robust and accurate, and is likely to remain in SAS service well into the next century.

Firing short, controlled bursts, the weapon has been used to deadly effect by SAS soldiers over the years. In 1971, for example, during the war against the People's Front for the Liberation of the Occupied Arabian Gulf (PFLOAG) in Oman, the SAS, working with units of the Sultan's Armed Forces (SAF) and *firqat* troops (irregular ex-communist fighters who had been trained by the SAS), was operating north of Taqa, Dhofar Province. The SAS had established a defensive position on the Jebel Aram using five ambush sites to stop any *adoo* (the name given to PFLOAG fighters) attacks. Three of these

Below: A Chinese Type 56 machine gun, a design based on the Soviet RPD series. Though now very old, it is still in service with the Chinese Army.

positions were manned by SAS soldiers and were equipped with GPMGs. The subsequent *adoo* attack was met by a hail of GPMG fire, the machine guns firing both tracer and standard ammunition. Under such a ferocious onslaught the *adoo* attack faltered, and eventually they retreated. It was used during the same campaign by Soldier 'I': 'I clipped a fresh belt of 200 rounds on to the old belt and began feeding the beast. Stream after stream of tracer zapped into the area of the [enemy] heavy machine gun, the sound of the GPMG drumming in my ears.' The war in Oman brought home the value of the GPMG to the SAS as a whole. Eleven years later Soldier 'I' was fighting in the Falklands: 'experience gained

in the Dhofar war had taught us how vital it was. We made sure we took every GPMG we could lay our hands on.'

In addition to being fitted with a bipod for the light role, the weapon can also be mounted on a tripod for the sustained-fire role.

Designation: L7A2
Calibre: 7.62mm
Weight: 10.9kg (in light role)
Length: 1232mm (light role); 1048mm (sustained-fire role)
Effective range: 1800m
Rate of fire: 750-1000 rounds per minute (cyclic)
Feed: belt
Muzzle velocity: 838 metres per second

Heckler & Koch 13E This German 5.56mm machine gun uses belt, M16 or double-drum magazines. It can fire three-round bursts as well as full-automatic and has the same mechanism as the G3 rifle. Currently under trial for the German Army, it is likely that the SAS, because it favours other Heckler & Koch guns, possesses some of these weapons.
Calibre: 5.56mm
Weight: 6kg (including bipod)
Length: 980mm
Effective range: 400m
Rate of fire: 750 rounds per minute (cyclic)
Feed: 25-round box magazine
Muzzle velocity: 950 metres per second

LSW The Light Support Weapon is the new light machine gun of the British Army. Essentially a heavy-barrelled version of the SA-80, the LSW is extremely accurate – especially in single-shot mode – and compact. Its lack of an interchangeable barrel, however, means it is unsuited to the sustained-fire role.
Designation: L86A1
Calibre: 5.56mm
Weight: 6.58kg
Length: 900mm
Effective range: 1000m
Rate of fire: 700-850 rounds per minute (cyclic)
Feed: 30-round box magazine
Muzzle velocity: 970 metres per second

SOVIET MACHINE GUNS
Most Soviet machine guns are robust, reliable weapons that are simple to fire and maintain in the field. Training in their use is given to all SAS soldiers. A sample is given below.

SGM An elderly design – it is no longer in frontline Russian service – though it is still in use in the many Third World states.
Calibre: 7.62mm
Weight: 13.6kg (empty)
Length: 1120mm
Effective range: 1000m
Rate of fire: 650 rounds per minute (cyclic)
Feed: 250-round pocketed belt
Muzzle velocity: 800 metres per second

RPK This is the Kalashnikov assault rifle turned into a light machine gun by giving it a longer barrel and a bipod. As such, it has all the virtues of its relation and is a good light squad automatic weapon.
Calibre: 7.62mm
Weight: 5kg (empty)
Length: 1035mm
Effective range: 800m
Rate of fire: 660 rounds per minute (cyclic)
Feed: 40-round box or 75-round drum magazine
Muzzle velocity: 732 metres per second

Left: The GPMG is one of the most valued weapons in the SAS armoury. Rugged and reliable, it has proved its worth in terrain ranging from the deserts of the Middle East to the cold of the Falklands.

Above: A water-cooled Vickers .303-inch machine gun in action in early 1943 in North Africa.

RPK-74 This is the RPK in 5.45mm calibre, i.e. the AK-74 adapted for the light machine gun role. It is believed that it has replaced the RPK in current Commonwealth of Independent States service. As yet there are no details available for this weapon.

Ultimax 100 A Singapore design, this weapon has a very soft recoil and is accurate and reliable. It is possible that the Regiment currently has some of these weapons.
Calibre: 5.56mm
Weight: 4.90kg (with bipod)
Length: 1024mm
Effective range: 1000m
Rate of fire: 400-600 rounds per minute (cyclic)
Feed: 100-round drum magazine; 20- or 30-round box magazine
Muzzle velocity: 970 metres per second

Vickers 'K' This weapon was mounted – usually in pairs – on World War II SAS jeeps. The Vickers was in fact an aircraft weapon that had originally been designed as an RAF observer's gun. The SAS usually loaded the magazines with a mixture of tracer, armour-piercing and explosive bullets, a cocktail useful in North Africa where the targets were parked enemy aircraft. The Vickers had a high rate of fire, a simple and robust mechanism and the 96-round drum magazine allowed long, sustained bursts. They didn't really have any bad points as such, although, as they were intended for aerial use, they were prone to overheating when fired for long periods (there was no slipstream to cool them).

The SAS used them to devastating effect throughout the war. At Sidi Haneish airfield in July 1942, for example, 18 SAS jeeps drove onto the airfield and riddled the parked aircraft with machine-gun fire. Some 40 German aircraft were destroyed in a matter of minutes, largely due to Vickers 'K' fire. The SAS did experience one drawback with the weapon: it had a habit of jamming at an inappropriate moment. In early July 1942, the SAS hit enemy airfields around Fuka, North Africa. Johnny Cooper, a young recruit to David Stirling's unit, was manning a single Vickers at the front of an SAS jeep. During a raid against one of these airfields Cooper's gun

jammed on the third drum, refusing to fire until it had cooled down.

A similar thing happened to Captain Derrick Harrison during Operation 'Kipling', a mission conducted by 1 SAS in central France in August and September 1944. While on routine patrol Harrison, accompanied by four men mounted on two heavily armed jeeps, was informed of a large German presence in the village of Les Ormes. The jeeps duly raced into the village square and started strafing the enemy soldiers, who happened to be SS. A firefight quickly developed, with Harrison firing twin Vickers machine guns at the front of one of the jeeps. However, his driver was then shot and his guns jammed. In fact all of the Vickers on his vehicle jammed and he was forced to abandon it and escape on the other one, the Vickers of which fortunately kept on firing. For his bravery Harrison was awarded the Military Cross.

Designation: Vickers GO
Calibre: .303-inch
Weight: 9.5kg
Length: 1016mm
Effective range: 1800m
Rate of fire: 1000 rounds per minute (cyclic)

Above: A World War II SAS jeep. Note the pair of Vickers 'K' machine guns mounted on the front.

Feed: 96-round drum magazine
Muzzle velocity: 745 metres per second

Vickers .303-inch machine gun An extremely reliable weapon – it could fire for hours without stoppages provided cooling water was available – the tripod-mounted Vickers was used by the SAS during World War II, particularly in Italy, France and Germany. Major Roy Farran, an officer with 2 SAS during the war, describes the Vickers thus: 'Skilled gunners could do things with it that were impossible for light machine-guns with a flatter trajectory. The technique of indirect fire with a machine gun, perfected by the Australians at Gaza in the First World War, is beyond the scope of more modern weapons.'

Calibre: .303-inch
Weight: 18.1kg
Length: 1156mm
Effective range: 2000m
Rate of fire: 450-500 rounds per minute (cyclic)
Feed: 250-round belt
Muzzle velocity: 744 metres per second

Section 4
HANDGUNS

The Special Air Service has used handguns in two capacities since its creation: as a side arm in World War II and, much more importantly, as a weapon for use during hostage-rescue/counter-terrorist operations, such as in the so-called 'Keeni Meeni' operations in Aden in the mid-1960s and, since the early 1970s, for undercover work against terrorists in Northern Ireland, both in Ulster and on the Continent.

The handgun's suitability for counter-terrorist work has been questioned in some quarters; after all, it could be argued that the submachine gun, with its heavy firepower and ability to place single shots accurately, has replaced the handgun. However, the latter is easier to wield one-handed and can be brought to bear on a target more quickly. The handgun is also generally reckoned to be an excellent weapon for rapid fire at less than 30m. Its draw-backs are that it is more difficult to operate and its high recoil reduces the accuracy of follow-on shots. However, the SAS has got around this problem to a great extent. Its soldiers are all highly trained: they can empty a magazine of 13 rounds from a High Power in under three seconds (the 'double tap', where two shots are fired in quick succession, has largely given way to sustained fire). Each soldier in a squadron under-going training in the 'Killing House', the building used to teach hostage-rescue and rapid entry techniques, will expend at least 5000 rounds of ammunition during the course.

The type of handguns used by the SAS has also changed since World War II. Formerly, the Regiment mainly used Webley revolvers; however, the semi-automatic handgun is now preferred as it holds 13 or more bullets compared to the revolver's six. The qualities that the SAS look for in a handgun are many and varied, though they all centre around first-time relia-bility and accuracy. The main attributes looked for are: reliability (in a hostage-rescue situation the action is usually over in seconds, therefore the first shot is vital); safety (there must be no risk of an accidental discharge before the assault); high-capacity magazines; compactness,

particularly for plain clothes work; ability to be operated with either the left or right hand; rapid magazine change function (something impossible with a revolver); speedy operation and aiming; and the capacity to work in adverse conditions.

Browning High Power The current handgun used by the SAS. The gun has been in military service since 1935, itself a testimony to the High Power's effectiveness, and it is reliable, accurate and simple to use. Though the Mark 2 model introduced in the mid-1980s received a hostile reception from the Regiment, the Mark 3 currently in use meets the SAS's exacting requirements. FN have now introduced the BDA double-action model which will probably replace the old single-action High Power. Double-action is a handgun firing mechanism that allows two methods of firing. First, manually cocking the hammer and pulling the trigger. Second, cocking and releasing the hammer by continuous pressure on the trigger.

The awesome power of the High Power was shown during the SAS operation – 'Flavius' – in Gibraltar on 8 March 1988. The shooting of three IRA terrorists – Mairead Farrell, Daniel McCann and Sean Savage – by four SAS soldiers at short ranges brought accusations of the Regiment operating a policy of shoot-to-kill against Irish Republican Army (IRA) suspects. Nevertheless, the incident proved the lethality of the High Power handgun. All the SAS soldiers were in plain clothes and had closed to within two or three metres of the suspects before opening fire. Farrell was hit five times – two to the neck and three in the torso – and the bullets that hit her in the back passed straight through her body. McCann was shot nine times and Savage was hit by no less than 15 9mm rounds. Both suffered horrific tissue damage.

Above right: The Browning High Power, a weapon used by the SAS for counter-terrorist operations. Below right: Familiarity with foreign-made guns is an integral part of SAS weapons training which encompasses models such as this Czech 75.

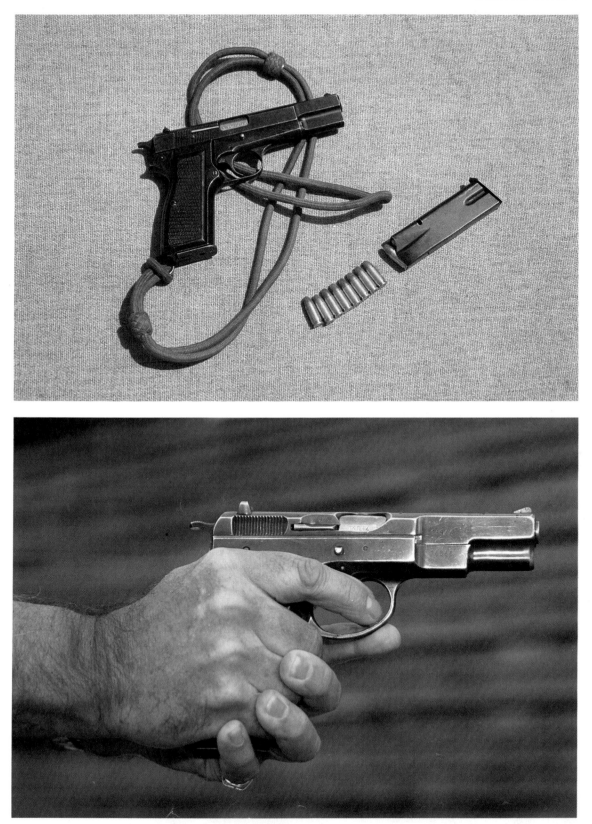

The Browning is carried by SAS troopers while on plain clothes duty in Ulster, as described by Soldier 'I': 'We were each armed with a 9-millimetre Browning automatic pistol. The four 13-round magazines gave me a feeling of security. The pistol grip of the 9-millimetre protruding from the Len Dixon holster dug uncomfortably into my ribs as we drove out through the heavily reinforced gate sangar...straight into the beating heart of Republican West Belfast.'

Designation: FN BDA (Browning Double-Action)
Calibre: 9mm
Weight: 905g (empty)
Length: 200mm
Effective range: 40m
Feed: 14-round box magazine
Muzzle velocity: 350 metres per second

Colt 1911A1 In many ways the ideal semi-automatic combat handgun provided adequate time is allowed for training in its use. Because the gun shoots a heavy load – .45-inch calibre – it jumps when it is fired and so takes time to learn to control and shoot it accurately. That said, the Colt is utterly reliable, easy to strip and operate and its round has awesome stopping power – when a person is hit they are knocked down and stay down!

Calibre: .45-inch
Weight: 1.13kg (empty)
Length: 219mm
Effective range: 40m
Feed: eight-round box magazine
Muzzle velocity: 253 metres per second

Glock handguns The most innovative and radical designs currently available in the handgun world belong to the Austrian firm Glock GmbH. These weapons are extremely lightweight – the receivers are made of high-resistant polymer material – which makes them ideal for SAS-type anti-terrorist operations. Glock handguns don't have a conventional safety catch; rather, safety is built into the trigger mechanism. The first pressure on the trigger disengages the trigger safety and cocks the striker, at the same time releasing two internal safety devices – the integral firing pin lock and the safety ramp. The second pressure releases the striker to fire the pistol.

Glock handguns are currently in service with the Austrian Army and in use with several NATO armies. As well as 9mm calibre, Glock is now making 0.4-inch, .45-inch and 10mm versions.

Glock 17
Type: semi-automatic handgun
Calibre: 9mm
Weight: 620g (empty)
Length: 188mm
Effective range: 50m
Feed: 17-round box magazine
Muzzle velocity: 360 metres per second

Glock 18 Based on the model 17, this weapon has a fire selector assembly and a larger magazine capacity, thus turning it into a machine pistol capable of automatic fire. It has been specially designed for units such as the SAS, whose soldiers may wish to fire trigger-controlled bursts from a lightweight handgun. This awesome firepower in a gun which has an empty weight of under one kilogram points the direction for future special forces handguns.

Type: semi- and full-automatic handgun
Calibre: 9mm
Weight: 636g (empty)
Length: 223mm
Effective range: 50m
Rate of fire: 1300 rounds per minute (cyclic)
Feed: 17-, 19- or 33-round box magazine
Muzzle velocity: 360 metres per second

Glock 19 Similar to the Glock 17 though smaller and more compact.
Type: semi-automatic handgun
Calibre: 9mm
Weight: 594g (empty)
Length: 177mm
Effective range: 50m
Feed: 15-round box magazine
Muzzle velocity: 360 metres per second

Luger This famous handgun of the German Army in World War II was used by SAS soldiers during the war when they happened to capture

Right: During CRW operations the Browning High Power is often used as a backup weapon, though it can be used first when only one hand is free.

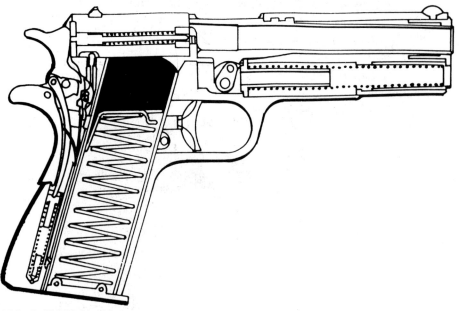

Colt .45-inch 1911A1 handgun

one while operating behind enemy lines. Surprisingly, the Luger was not an ideal combat pistol because it was sensitive to variations in ammunition. It could not fire British rounds, for example. This meant it had limitations in the field; after all, during wartime conditions a handgun should be able to fire any ammunition that is available.

Designation: Parabellum-Pistole Modell 1908
Calibre: 9mm
Weight: 870g (empty)
Length: 223mm
Effective range: 40m
Feed: eight-round detachable box magazine
Muzzle velocity: 350 metres per second

SIG-Sauer handguns The handguns produced by the Swiss firm SIG-Sauer are among the most reliable weapons in the world. They have recently entered SAS service and it is not hard to discern why: the Royal Canadian Mounted Police carried out tests on the P 226 gun firing 10 test weapons and discharging 150,000 rounds. The rate of malfunction was 0.007 of one per cent and none was due to the failure of parts of magazines. With this kind of reliability they are ideal for

Special Air Service operations, where the first shot counts every time.

SIG guns are also extremely good for accuracy, speed of aiming and speed of operation. The P 228 is very compact, making it easy to conceal. All the following models have the double-action trigger device and a magazine catch which can be reversed to provide greater convenience and ease of operation for left-handed shooters. SIG handguns are currently used by the FBI and US presidential bodyguards. The only drawback concerning SIG handguns is their price – they are expensive. However, this tends not to be a problem for the SAS, as it has its own funds as well as money allocated to it by the Ministry of Defence.

Right: Early in 1991, it was announced in the British press that the Swiss firm SIG-Sauer had sold a number of its handguns to the UK Ministry of Defence following competitive trials against all comparable available rivals. The models bought included the P 228 (top) and the P 226 (bottom). It seems certain that the SAS has taken delivery of a number of these excellent handguns and will employ them for counter-terrorist missions.

P 226

Type: single- or double-action handgun
Calibre: 9mm
Weight: 750g (empty)
Length: 196mm
Effective range: 50m
Feed: 15- or 20-round magazine
Muzzle velocity: 350 metres per second

P 228

Type: single- or double-action handgun
Calibre: 9mm
Weight: 830g (empty)
Length: 180mm
Effective range: 50m
Feed: 13-round magazine
Muzzle velocity: 345 metres per second

Webley The Webley range of handguns was used by SAS soldiers, specifically officers, during World War II. Though they would be unsuitable for today's counter-terrorist operations, Webley revolvers were very strong and very accurate. They were, in addition, put together with a very high standard of workmanship and materials. In their day they were the best available; indeed, the Webley is still widely used by police and military forces throughout the world, particularly by those forces which were originally equipped and trained by the British.

Designation: Pistol, Webley, Mark 6
Calibre: .455-inch
Weight: 1.09kg (empty)
Length: 286mm
Effective range: 40m
Feed: six-round cylinder magazine
Muzzle velocity: 199 metres per second

Right: French SAS troops on parade during the latter stages of World War II. The officers and NCOs are wearing holsters which contain Webley revolvers. Superbly made and extremely rugged, Webleys were at the time the best in the world. Such revolvers are now outmoded, however. The Webley held six rounds in its cylindrical magazine, whereas modern semi-automatic handguns have magazines which hold 12 or more rounds. This makes them ideal for SAS contacts with terrorists, where individual troopers are taught to put down the target with sustained firepower.

Section 5
SHOTGUNS

The Special Air Service first employed the shotgun as a close-quarter weapon for jungle fighting. During the Regiment's campaign in Malaya (1948-60), the semi-automatic shotgun was used to great effect by individual soldiers, particularly lead scouts. Sergeant Bob Turnbull, for example, became a legendary figure on account of his expert tracking skills and his use with a Browning auto-loader shotgun. On one occasion, while tracking Communist Terrorists, his patrol was suddenly confronted by one of the enemy some five metres away. Turnbull's reactions were so quick that he managed to fire three shots which killed the terrorist before the latter managed to fire once.

A typical engagement in Malaya using a shotgun is described by Lieutenant-Colonel Johnny Cooper thus: 'They [the SAS patrol] heard movement in the thick bamboo further up the mountain and quickly moved into an ambush position. [Sergeant] Levett ordered the signaller, who was only armed with an M1 Carbine, to shoot the first CT [Communist Terrorist] who appeared, while he would use his pump-action shotgun loaded with 12-bore SG shot to spray the ground behind. Slowly the noise of movement increased and the first enemy scout appeared. The signaller opened fire, but his high velocity .30 calibre bullet failed to hit a vital part. Levett finished him off with his first shot and then pumped the remaining eight rounds into the jungle beyond. There they found three bodies, torn to pieces by the SG shot.'

The SAS now uses shotguns for counter-terrorist operations, specifically blowing door hinges prior to an assault team's entry into a room to either kill or capture terrorists and/or to free hostages. The Regiment no longer employs shotguns for jungle warfare, modern automatic weapons having made their use unnecessary. In general there are several problems with using the shotgun for military purposes. The Browning auto-loaders used in the 1950s and 1960s, for example, were never designed for the rough and tumble of jungle (or any other) warfare. They were first and foremost a hunting weapon, and in

such a role they gave no trouble. However, in a war situation they tended to become unreliable unless they were nursed very carefully. For this reason they tended to quickly disappear from the SAS jungle armoury.

Despite its unsuitability for field operations, the shotgun has remained an important part of the counter-terrorist armoury. This is because shotguns can fire a wide variety of cartridges – buckshot, armour-piercing, Hatton rounds (designed to blow off door hinges without injury to the occupants of the room), CS gas to name but a few – and thus the firer can use cartridges for the particular situation in hand. Should the shotgun need to be used in an anti-personnel role, then it has formidable stopping power. The effect of a cartridge containing around 10 soft lead balls, for example, can be likened to a nine-round burst from a submachine gun (because of the spread effect of the shot they are never used if the room contains hostages).

Browning auto-loader Used by the SAS in Malaya, it was in fact a hunting gun and one really unsuited to jungle warfare. Nevertheless, with maintenance it worked well enough.
Calibre: 12-gauge
Weight: 4.1kg
Length: 1035mm
Effective range: 50m
Feed: five rounds in internal magazine plus one in the chamber

Franchi shotguns It was the Franchi Special Purpose Automatic Shotgun (SPAS) 12 which introduced the concept of the purpose-built police shotgun. It is a formidable weapon that is capable of semi- or full-automatic fire, as well as being a pump-action shotgun should the firer desire it. Franchi shotguns are robust and reliable, and are ideally suited to Counter Revolutionary Warfare (CRW) operations.

Right: The Remington 870 pump-action shotgun, seen here, is used by the SAS for effecting entry into rooms during counter-terrorist operations.

SPAS 12 This shotgun has a skeleton butt which has a special device that allows one-handed firing if required. The barrel spreads pellets to a 900mm diameter at 40m and greater at longer ranges. This means the firer has only to take a rough aim to hit the target – a great bonus in a darkened room full of terrorists. Set on automatic fire, the SPAS 12 fires a devastating four shots a second. In addition, a special device can be fitted onto the muzzle which produces an instantaneous spread of pellets – useful for indoor firing.

Type: semi- or full-automatic pump-action shotgun
Calibre: 12-gauge
Weight: 4.20kg
Length: 930mm; 710mm (stock folded)
Effective range: 50m
Rate of fire: 24-30 rounds per minute (practical)
Feed: seven-round internal magazine
Muzzle velocity: depends on type of round being used

SPAS 15 The main feature of this shotgun is its box magazine which replaced the SPAS 12's tubular magazine. This weapon is capable of both pump-action (rounds are loaded by manually operating the foregrip/pumping handle beneath the barrel) and semi-automatic fire.

Calibre: 12-gauge
Weight: 3.90kg (without magazine)
Length: 915mm

Effective range: 50m
Feed: six-round box magazine

Remington 870 The main SAS assault shotgun, the 870 has been widely used during anti-terrorist operations in Ulster, specifically to blow off door hinges prior to the arrest of IRA suspects (it is also used in the same capacity for hostage-rescue work). Soldier 'I' used a Remington in Ulster: 'The safety-catch on the Remington came off as I hit the third floor and made for the target door. Number one and number two were already in position at the hinges, waiting for the door to swing open. I squeezed the trigger on the shotgun. The cartridge hammered through the Yale lock, splintering the wood surround into a thousand slivers.' Because it was built from the start as a riot gun and not as a hunting weapon, it is much more robust than the average shotgun.

Type: pump-action shotgun
Calibre: 12-gauge
Weight: 3.60kg
Length: 1060mm
Effective range: 40m
Feed; seven-shot tubular magazine

Below: An SAS patrol hunts for CTs in Malaya, mid-1950s. The soldier in the foreground is armed with a Browning pump-action shotgun.

Section 6
SNIPER RIFLES

SAS snipers are trained to fulfil two main, and very different, roles. The first is to operate in the field during a conventional war. This requires the individual trooper to hit a head-sized target with a first-round shot out to a range of around 300m and a body-sized target at a range of 600-1000m. However, the longer the range the greater the possibility that more than one shot will be required, thus increasing the chances of the sniper's detection. The sniper therefore has to combine his marksmanship skills with a high degree of fieldcraft and concealment.

Second, SAS snipers have to operate in Counter Revolutionary Warfare (CRW). This type of sniping requires slightly different skills, as the marksmen are usually static and their concealment is not always essential. In addition, the engagement ranges are always shorter, for example, around 100m. However, while a battlefield sniper is usually successful if he just wounds his target, the counter-terrorist marksman must kill with his first shot, which can be fired after hours of waiting (though of course the prospects of a first-hit kill are much greater at close ranges).

The sniper rifles currently and previously used by the SAS have been used in both the above two roles. The models currently available are in fact much better than those employed by the Regiment up to the Falklands War of 1982; indeed, early SAS rifles were merely bolt-action models equipped with sniper sights and modified to fire 7.62mm ammunition. Thus the L42A1 was a .303-inch Lee-Enfield bolt-action rifle with sights and a heavier barrel. However, the adoption by Western armies of rifles firing the 5.56mm round prompted a rethink concerning military and police sniper rifles. The smaller calibre ammunition, because of its lack of range, was regarded as being generally ill-suited to sniper work and so attention was focused on rifles developed for hunting and target shooting as these had many of the attributes favourable for sniper use: bolt-action, match-weight barrels, synthetic and adjustable butts, bipods and adjustable triggers. The new Special Air Service

and British Army sniper rifle, the L96A1, has all these features.

One interesting feature of modern sniping is the choice of calibres currently available. The SAS uses the 7.62mm L96A1 for its sniper rifle. However, by using a larger calibre, 0.5-inch for example, it is possible to hit targets beyond a range of 1000m and also to disable objects such as vehicles, armoured personnel carriers, helicopters, parked aircraft and fuel dumps. At the other end of the scale, there are several advantages in using 5.56mm ammunition, especially for counter-terrorist work: minimum recoil means it is easier to shoot more accurately and the lighter round is less likely to shoot through structural materials. However, there is no evidence as yet to suggest the SAS will start using 5.56mm sniper rifles.

Accuracy International PM This is the British Army's new sniper rifle. It has superb accuracy, though no more than other models currently available. The PM has a plastic stock, a light bipod and a monopod in the butt, which allows the rifle to be laid on the target for long periods without the firer having to support the weight of the weapon. The sights are Schmidt and Bender 6x42 which allow accurate fire out to a range of 1000m. Accuracy International also produce a silenced version of the rifle which, using special subsonic ammunition, is accurate to a range of 300m.

Type: bolt-action sniper rifle
Designation: L96A1
Calibre: 7.62mm
Weight: 6.50kg
Length: 1124-1194mm
Effective range: 1000m
Feed: 10-round box magazine
Muzzle velocity: 914 metres per second

Above right: The L42A1 sniper rifle, which combined the attributes of a sniper rifle with the ruggedness of the Lee-Enfield .303-inch rifle.
Below right: The new SAS sniper rifle, the 7.62mm Accuracy International PM.

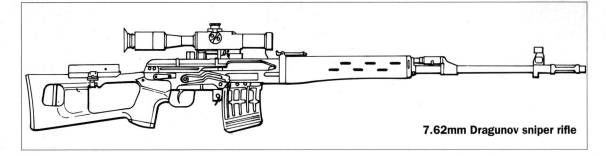

7.62mm Dragunov sniper rifle

Dragunov This Soviet sniper rifle is a semi-automatic model which has a bolt system based on the AK-47. It is equipped with the PSO-1 telescopic sight that gives a magnification of times four. As it is, or was, the main sniper rifle of the Red Army, the SAS is trained in its use. It is reportedly an accurate weapon, though rather cumbersome.

Type: semi-automatic sniper rifle
Designation: SVD
Calibre: 7.62mm
Weight: 4.30kg
Length: 1225mm
Effective range: 800m
Feed: 10-round detachable box magazine
Muzzle velocity: 830 metres per second

L42A1 A conversion from the .303-inch No 4 rifle, this weapon has all the virtues of the basic Lee-Enfield design, allied to a heavy barrel and the 7.62mm NATO cartridge, and was used extensively by the SAS, particularly in Oman during the 1970s. It is a very sound gun, though not in the same accuracy league as modern systems. Nevertheless, the SAS was using it to good effect right up to the 1982 Falklands War.

Type: bolt-action sniper rifle
Calibre: .303-inch
Weight: 4.43kg
Length: 1181mm
Effective range: 800m
Feed: 10-round box magazine
Muzzle velocity: 838 metres per second

SSG 69 Before the introduction of the Accuracy International PM, the SAS experimented with a number of sniper rifles, among which was the Austrian SSG 69. A gun noted for its reliability and superb accuracy, the SSG 69's stock can be adjusted for length by the removal or addition of a butt pad. In addition, the length and weight of the trigger pull can both be adjusted.

Type: bolt-action sniper rifle
Calibre: 7.62mm
Weight: 4.60kg (empty)
Length: 1140mm
Effective range: 800m
Feed: five-round rotary magazine
Muzzle velocity: 860 metres per second

SSG 3000 This bipod-equipped sniper rifle, produced by the Swiss firm SIG Sauer, is an example of the superb European models currently available. The SSG 3000 is cast in the familiar SIG mould, being extremely robust and accurate.

Type: bolt-action sniper rifle
Calibre: .308-inch
Weight: 6.20kg (empty)
Length: 1180mm
Effective range: 650m
Feed: five-round magazine
Muzzle velocity: 750 metres per second

Tikka M55 Another sniper rifle that the SAS used before the adoption of the L96A1. This Finnish-built gun can fire a variety of different calibre ammunition.

Type: bolt-action sniper rifle
Designation: M55 Super Sporter
Calibre: various (.223-inch, .243-inch, 7mm)
Weight: 3.27kg
Length: 1010mm
Effective range: 550m
Feed: four-round magazine
Muzzle velocity: 900 metres per second

Right: All snipers must be highly proficient in fieldcraft skills which include camouflaging themselves and their weapons.

WEAPON SIGHTS

The range of sights currently available is immense and therefore it is impossible to give a comprehensive list of all the main systems accessible to units such as the SAS. Thus the models listed below are intended to give an indication only of the various sights in production.

Optical and telescopic sights Standard-issue optical sights, such as the British Sight Unit Small Arms Trilux (SUSAT) fitted to the SA-80 assault rifle, can improve the firer's shooting. However, they can also hinder target location, and this is especially true for units such as the SAS which operates in small groups and usually has quick, violent contacts with the enemy. Telescopic sights for sniper employment usually give a magnification of between four and six, though some zoom scopes can give a magnification of ten. However, they can only be used during daylight and so are not really suited to hostage-rescue operations where an assault may take place at night.

SUSAT Fitted to SA-80 rifles, this sight can also be mounted on a wide range of rifles, machine guns and recoilless rifles. It gives a times four magnification.

ZF10 X 42 telescopic sight Produced by the German firm M Hensoldt and Sohne Optische Werke, this sight is intended for shooting up to a range of 1000m. The sight gives a times 10 magnification and all its surfaces have a reflection-reducing coating.

Infrared sights These work by the emission of beams in the infrared wavelength which 'illuminate' the target area and thus give the firer an image to aim a shot at. The main disadvantage with standard infrared sights is that the emission can be easily detected by the target, and counter-snipers can use a passive detector to locate the source of the illuminating beam. The latest passive infrared sights, called 'thermal imaging' sights, are much better, though rather bulky for field use. An example of this type of sight is the Short-Range Thermal Sight produced by the American firm Magnavox Electro-Optical Systems. It is a passive infrared imaging rifle sight designed mainly for use on the M16 rifle, though it can be adapted to fit on other weapons. It allows the firer to detect a target in total darkness.

Image intensifying sights The mechanics of these sights are rather complicated. A gross but understandable simplification of how they work would be: they take the light that is available and intensify it thousands of times to enhance visibility. In fact, the latest image intensifying sights can work in virtually no light at all. Needless to say they are extremely expensive and complicated, but they do allow a sniper or other firer to operate in low light conditions.

Models currently available include the Orion 80 passive night sight produced by the German firm Electro GmbH which can be fitted to Heckler & Koch MP5 submachine guns and gives a times four magnification. The British firm Davin Optical produces the IRS 218 night rifle scope, a system designed for the battlefield which gives a magnification of 2.8 and can be fitted to all service rifles.

Laser sights With these systems the firer usually wears night vision goggles which can discern an otherwise invisible white beam emitted from a weapon mounting a laser aiming device. The American firm Litton System Inc., for example, produces the AIM-1D/DLR laser aiming sight which allows a person wearing night vision goggles to aim a weapon accurately. The Dutch firm Oldelft markets the TM-007, an infrared laser pointer designed for close-range combat to be used in conjunction with night vision goggles. These are just two examples of the range currently available to elite units such as the Special Air Service.

Above right: An SA-80 fitted with a SAWES (Small Arms Weapons Effect Simulation) sight.
Below right: A modern image intensifying sight.

SUPPORT WEAPONS

SAS troops are trained in the use of a wide range of support weapons ranging from anti-tank guns to mortars and grenade launchers. These systems are significant force multipliers for small-sized teams tasked with sabotage and hit-and-run missions behind enemy lines.

The need to move over great distances, often at speed, means SAS soldiers often cannot carry heavy weapons such as large mortars and field pieces. That said, the Regiment has employed many types of support weapons in its campaigns since its creation. Even when operating behind enemy lines, such as in France in 1944, SAS units have been equipped with artillery pieces and mortars, usually to defend static positions. And these weapons have often been used with great expertise by individual soldiers. At the Battle of Mirbat in July 1972, for example, SAS troopers manned and fired a 25-pounder field gun with a precision and skill that would have been the envy of any gunner from the Royal Artillery.

What does the SAS use support weapons for? Just that – support. They can add substantially to the firepower of an attack or, conversely, beef up the defence. As the following text illustrates, SAS teams have used a variety of support weapons with devastating effect since 1941.

A Milan anti-tank weapon in action. Though its lethality cannot be doubted – the missile can penetrate up to 1060mm of armour – its weight largely precludes it being used by SAS foot patrols.

Section 1
MORTARS

The traditional role of the mortar is to provide close support to an infantry section, company or battalion (such support can also be provided by artillery, though the latter is seldom present during SAS actions, especially if they take place behind enemy lines). Historically mortars have been used to give weight to an SAS attack. During the assault on the Jebel Akhdar, Oman, in January 1959, A Squadron used three-inch mortars during the capture of an enemy stronghold called 'Sabrina'. It also used them to drop smoke onto enemy positions before the assault to enable RAF Shackleton bombers to pinpoint enemy locations prior to pounding them with 1000lb bombs.

During the 1982 Falklands War, mortars were used during the Pebble Island raid. With their comparative lightness and firepower, mortars will undoubtedly remain in the SAS armoury for many years to come.

Two-inch mortar A Spanish design, this weapon was adopted by the British Army in 1937 and only went out of service in 1980, being replaced by the 51mm mortar. It was used by the SAS in World War II because it was light, handy, reliable and an excellent platoon support weapon. The only disadvantage, one universal to all mortars, was the burden of having to carry its ammunition around (the latter was usually carried in boxes, each containing three bombs).

The two-inch could fire high explosive rounds, smoke and flares, the latter being useful for night fighting. It had a trigger firing mechanism, making it an ideal weapon for firing at angles near to the horizontal.
Weight: 4.10kg
Maximum range: 457m
Bomb weight: 1.02kg (high explosive)

Three-inch mortar A British weapon developed in the 1920s for the infantry so the then-existing Light Regiments of the Royal Artillery (which were using 3.7-inch pack howitzers) could be reorganised into the field role and given larger guns. It was used extensively by the

SAS during World War II and in Aden (1964-67) and Oman (1970-76). It was accurate, though rather heavy to be manhandled, and its range at first left a lot to be desired (though this was later rectified with an improved barrel and bomb). It continued in British service until the late 1970s, being replaced by the 81mm mortar.

There are many examples of its employment by the SAS in World War II, though one will serve to illustrate its use. During Operation 'Houndsworth', a mission conducted by men from 1 SAS in eastern France between June and September 1944, a party was detailed to attack a refinery near the town of Autun. The SAS set up a three-inch mortar on a hill overlooking the plant, the moonlit night giving ample opportunity to sight the weapon correctly. The mortar was directed by Alec Muirhead, an expert who had fought with the Special Raiding Squadron earlier in Italy (the Special Raiding Squadron was in fact 1 SAS which had been temporarily renamed). He began firing at 0200 hours, at first using smoke bombs to bed in the baseplate and provide visual sighting. The incendiary and high explosive soon followed, the rounds slamming into the refinery. The latter was soon engulfed in flames, its German guards having no idea of the whereabouts of the attackers. The SAS team, having been entirely successful, then packed up the mortar and departed.
Weight: 57.2kg
Maximum range: 2515m
Bomb weight: 4.54kg (high explosive)

4.2-inch mortar Used by the Special Air Service in World War II, this British weapon was really too heavy to be manhandled and was predominantly an artillery weapon (a wheeled baseplate was eventually developed for it). Its bomb had good range, accuracy and firepower, though the fins often split when fired which had

Above right: A British three-inch mortar pounds German positions in early 1945. This weapon was widely used by the SAS during World War II.
Below right: The British Army 51mm mortar.

a tendency of reducing the weapon's overall range and effectiveness.
Weight: 599kg
Maximum range: 3749m
Bomb weight: 9.07kg

51mm mortar This appeared in the 1970s and has become a simple and useful weapon currently in use with the SAS and British Army. It is essentially an updated version of the two-inch mortar, though lighter and more accurate. The 51mm mortar can fire high explosive, illuminating and smoke rounds.
Weight: 6.28kg
Maximum range: 800m
Bomb weight: 0.92kg (high explosive)

81mm mortar A British weapon that is at the forefront of mortar design. It is extremely accurate due to its well-engineered barrel and the streamlined bomb which has a plastic sealing ring on it so the propelling gas is trapped behind the bomb and forces it up and out, unlike earlier mortars which allowed the gas to escape. This means the bomb is centred better in the bore and doesn't yaw from side to side so much as it leaves the barrel, all of which aids accuracy.

Currently in service with the SAS, it was used by the Regiment during the Pebble Island raid in the Falklands War. The raid took place on the night of 14/15 May 1982 and was designed to destroy those Argentinian aircraft using the island's airstrip. The latter were regarded as a potential threat to the main British landings that were due to take place at San Carlos Water on 21 May.

D Squadron, 22 SAS, was tasked with carrying out the action and so, on 11 May, personnel from the squadron's Boat Troop were put ashore to reconnoitre the area. On the evening of the 14th, Sea King helicopters of 846 Squadron took off from the carrier *Hermes* carrying the SAS soldiers. The troops were landed some six kilometres from the airstrip and undertook a forced march the rest of the way, each man carrying two bombs for the 81mm mortars. The attack went in, supported by the mortars and naval gunfire, and some 11 enemy aircraft were destroyed, the SAS suffering only two men wounded.

A recent addition to the armoury of the 81mm mortar is Merlin, a terminally-guided anti-armour bomb which can be used with any 81mm calibre mortar. The bomb is launched in the traditional way, after which it deploys six rear-mounted fins to provide aerodynamic stability, and then four canard fins to give directional control. The bomb's miniature active millimetric seeker then switches on and searches for, first, moving targets and then stationary ones. The seeker scans an area 300m by 300m and then, after acquiring a target, the guidance system ensures impact with the most vulnerable sections on the top of the armoured vehicle. Though Merlin is not yet in service (full-scale production is anticipated for 1993), when it is deployed it will be a potent weapon.
Weight: 37.85kg
Maximum range: 5650m
Bomb weight: 4.2kg (high explosive)

Chinese 60mm mortar This weapon was used by *firqat* (ex-communist Dhofari fighters who were trained by the SAS) units during the campaign in Oman (1970-76). Most of the *firqat* soldiers were former fighters with the People's Front for the Liberation of the Occupied Arabian Gulf. As such, they had received training in the use of Chinese and Soviet weapons – both supported the PFLOAG in its efforts to bring down the regime of, first, Sultan Said bin Taimur and then his son, Qaboos. Many *firqat* fighters brought their weapons with them when they switched sides, including the 60mm mortar. The Type 31 was a copy of the US 60mm M2, though it was, like most Chinese copies, inferior in quality.
Weight: 20.2kg
Maximum range: 1530m
Bomb weight: 1.2kg

Right: An 81mm mortar in action. This weapon is one of the most successful mortar designs in the world, having entered service with the US Army and the armed forces of 15 other countries. In addition to being fired from a prepared position on the ground, the 81mm can also be fired from the FV 432 armoured personnel carrier.
Overleaf: An 81mm mortar firing the Merlin terminally-guided anti-armour bomb.

Section 2
ANTI-TANK WEAPONS

It might at first seem strange that the SAS should have a use for anti-tank weapons (which are often bulky pieces of kit). That said, during World War II the Regiment employed them against light armour, as area defence weapons, and during ambushes. The modern-day SAS is not tasked with stopping tanks or establishing heavily defended positions in a conventional battle scenario. It would not, therefore, use the heavier class of anti-tank weapons such as TOW.

Anti-tank weapons, including light field guns, did play a part in SAS operations in France after D-Day, when many bases were established behind enemy lines. These sites, often shared with the French Resistance, the *Maquis*, were often difficult to hide from the Germans because of the number of enemy patrols and, more serious, traitors in the ranks of the *Maquis*. Therefore, when they were discovered the presence of an anti-tank gun and some mortars did help to stiffen the defence. Today, SAS units usually travel light and would therefore stick to man-portable anti-armour weapons such as the LAW family or light rocket launchers.

Six-pounder anti-tank gun This British weapon was used in World War II from 1941 onwards and remained in service until the late 1950s. Originally a Royal Artillery gun, it was then distributed to infantry support companies and widely used by them in the North African desert. The six-pounder was accurate, tough and performed very well in the anti-armour role because it fired a fairly wide range of ammunition which was continually being improved. The first gun to stop a German Tiger tank in North Africa, for example, was a six-pounder. It also had the advantage of being light enough to be easily manhandled by its crew when required.

The SAS used the gun most notably in France in 1944, for example during Operation 'Houndsworth' between June and September. The SAS and *Maquis* had established a large base in wooded countryside to the west of Dijon. Eventually the SAS built up a strength of nearly 150 officers and men in the area – in addition to *Maquis* fighters – and their weapons included two six-pounder guns. The commander of the operation, Major Bill Fraser, A Squadron, 1 SAS, had placed the artillery to cover his headquarters in the woods. On 3 August, German troops attacked several *Maquis* positions in the woods but were beaten off with the help of one of the six-pounders, the enemy being surprised and demoralised by the presence of artillery.

Calibre: 57mm
Armour penetration: 130mm at 915m

25-pounder field gun The most memorable example of this World War II-vintage weapon in SAS use occurred at the Battle of Mirbat on 19 July 1972. The heroic exploits of two Fijians from the Regiment – Corporal Labalaba and Trooper Savesaki – while manning the gun during the action have entered SAS legend. The 25-pounder was in a gun-pit beside the Gendarmerie Fort. The *adoo*, the communist guerrillas of the People's Front for the Liberation of the Occupied Arabian Gulf, who numbered some 250, correctly perceived that the key to the battle was the fort and the 25-pounder gun in the pit beside it. They therefore concentrated their attacks on both, though they had not reckoned on the efforts of Labalaba. Loading shell after shell into the breech, the giant Fijian was seemingly beating off the hordes of Arab fighters single-handedly (though in fact he was assisted by an Omani gunner), as witnessed by Soldier 'I': 'Laba worked feverishly to load and blast the big gun at the fanatical enemy struggling through the fence only metres away. The twenty-five-pounder was traversed through forty-five degrees and used in the direct-fire role, dealing death at point-blank range. The breech detonations threw up clouds of cordite. A pall of acrid fumes hovered over the firing mechanism, growing bigger by the minute.'

Above right: A six-pounder in action at Arnhem.
Below right: The 25-pounder field gun.

Above: In service for nearly 30 years, the Carl Gustav is still a very effective weapon against armoured vehicles and enemy bunkers.

As the battle progressed Labalaba was hit in the chin by an AK-47 round. At this moment Savesaki lost radio contact with him and, fearing for his countryman's life, volunteered to go to the gun-pit with medical aid. Captain Mike Kealy, the SAS commander, agreed and Savesaki raced across 600m of open, bullet-swept ground, reaching the field gun breathless but unharmed. The 25-pounder continued to belch death as the *adoo* attack continued. Machine-gun fire from the 'Batt House' (Kealy's HQ) assisted the efforts of the gunners. However, Savesaki received a shot in the shoulder and, much worse, Labalaba was then killed.

Kealy himself decided to investigate and, taking Trooper Tobin with him, set off for the gun-pit. Reaching their objective, Tobin took over, manning the 25-pounder before being mortally wounded himself. The *adoo* attack continued, unabated in its ferocity. Kealy ordered the other SAS men to bring down mortar and machine-gun fire on his position in a last, desperate attempt to beat off the enemy, whose dead and wounded now littered the area. Relief was at hand, however, for at that moment Omani Strikemaster jets screamed overhead and began pouring cannon fire into the *adoo*. One hour later, SAS reinforcements arrived and launched a counterattack, driving the enemy back. The Battle of Mirbat was over. Both the battle and the 25-pounder gun passed into SAS folklore.

The gun itself was an excellent weapon, being accurate and reliable, and had a long barrel life. It was also very flexible, performing both as a gun or howitzer as required, and in North Africa in World War II it was a formidable anti-tank weapon. It could also fire a wide range of ammunition (the addition of a muzzle brake allowed it to fire anti-armour rounds) and its gun platform allowed all-round fire. The 25-pounder was the best divisional weapon of World War II and, as illustrated at Mirbat, it was used well into the post-war era; indeed, some are still in Indian and Pakistani service.

Calibre: 87.6mm

Range: 12,253m

Bazooka The World War II bazooka was an American 2.36-inch model which survived through to the Korean War (1950-53) and was then replaced by the 3.5-inch version. It was used by the SAS during the campaign in northwest Europe (1944-45), being frequently carried on jeeps as a support weapon. It was an accurate, light and easy to use weapon, and later versions could be broken in half which made them easier to carry. It did have a major drawback, however: a terrific flame signature which made the user a prime target for enemy machine gunners and snipers. Nevertheless, it was a good anti-tank weapon which could knock out most German main battle tanks. Bazookas were used by 2 SAS during Operation 'Tombola' (March-April 1945) in northern Italy, most notably during an attack on a German headquarters, as described by the SAS commander, Major Roy Farran: 'Bullets whistled over our heads, as if the Germans could see us, which was impossible. Even mortars added their thuds to the general racket and, between the rattle of small-arms fire

at Villa Calvi above, I heard the thump of a bazooka [used to blow in the HQ's front door].'
Calibre: 60mm
Range: 594m (maximum)
Armour penetration: 119.4mm

Carl Gustav An anti-tank weapon currently in service with the SAS, the Carl Gustav is reliable, robust and accurate. In addition, it is versatile enough to fire anti-personnel, smoke and illuminating rounds in the support role. Designed to be used by a two-man team – one fires the gun and the other carries the ammunition and loads – the weapon is generally well liked by servicemen. It's flexibility may be judged by the exploits of a Royal Marine carrying one during the Falklands War. He first brought down an Argentinian helicopter and then blew a hole in an enemy destroyer.

Below: The replacement for the Carl Gustav, the LAW 80. The system is rather awkward to carry, a factor that does not endear it to the SAS.

The weapon has been in SAS service for some time, being used during the campaign on the Jebel Akhdar, northern Oman, in late 1958 and early 1959. Its use was vividly described by an SAS machine gunner taking part in the conflict: 'first thing in the morning, several men [enemy guerrillas] came out of the cave and were about to start leading the donkeys out. Whereupon, three rounds rapid from the Carl Gustav went straight in the middle and whoof, they blew the cave in and a fair number of them to pieces.'

Designation: RCL Carl Gustav M2
Calibre: 84mm
Weight: 14.2kg
Length: 1130mm
Effective range: 450m (anti-tank); 1000m (high explosive)
Armour penetration: 400mm

LAW 80 A replacement for the Carl Gustav, this is a one-shot short-range anti-tank weapon designed to defeat modern main battle tanks up to a range of 500m. Its warhead is very effective and the Light Anti-tank Weapon (LAW) has an aiming rifle built-in which means the first-round hit probability is higher than usual for this class of weapon. However, it does have an awful firing signature: a loud bang and a cloud of smoke

Above: Milan. Used by the SAS during the Falklands War, it is a potent anti-tank weapon.

which can be seen a long way off. This, together with the fact that the system is rather heavy and awkward, means LAW 80 would probably not accompany SAS teams on long-range patrols.

Calibre: 94mm
Weight: 10kg
Length: 1m (folded); 1.5m (extended)
Effective range: 500m
Armour penetration: 700mm

M72 This American weapon was used to devastating effect by the SAS during the Pebble Island raid in the Falklands War, when members of D Squadron destroyed Argentine aircraft on the airstrip with a lethal combination of mortar and small-arms fire, explosive charges and 66mm anti-armour rounds.

The M72 is a throw-away rocket launcher which is light – its weight means several can be carried by one soldier – and accurate. Although the original version is now only effective against light armour, the current model will defeat armour up to a thickness of 335mm, has increased range, and is also capable of taking out strongpoints. Like most light anti-armour weapons, the M72 has a prominent firing

Above: The M72 is ideally suited to special forces operations, being light, accurate and deadly.

signature, though in the final analysis it is a reliable, versatile and effective weapon. The M72 fires a rocket mounting a High Explosive Anti-Tank (HEAT) warhead.

Calibre: 66mm
Weight: 2.36kg (complete assembly)
Length: 655mm (closed); 893mm (extended)
Effective range: 150m (moving targets); 300m (stationary targets)
Armour penetration: 335mm

Milan This anti-tank weapon is designed to be used by infantry from a defensive position. It fires a Semi-Automatic Command to Line-Of-Sight (SACLOS) wire-guided missile and so the operator has to keep the cross-hairs of the sights on the target throughout its flight. Accurate, reliable and having good armour penetration capabilities, Milan also has an excellent night sight. The whole system is heavy, though, and so it is highly unlikely that SAS parties on deep-penetration missions would carry Milans with them. However, if they were establishing large bases behind enemy lines, a modern equivalent of those set up in France in 1944, for example, then Milan positions would probably be set up.

In addition, the Regiment did use Milans during the 1982 Falklands War, when soldiers from D Squadron made a diversionary attack on Argentinian positions on 20 May to cover the main British landings at San Carlos Water. In this situation the SAS needed the heavy firepower and bunker-busting capabilities of the weapon. Significantly, however, the party, which was also armed with mortars, did not have to travel far to the target on foot (they were dropped off by Sea King helicopters) and so the weight of the system was not a factor.

Weight: 16.4kg (missile weighs 6.65kg)
Length: 900mm
Effective range: 2000m
Armour penetration: 1060mm

PIAT The Projector, Infantry, Anti-Tank Mk 1 was used by the SAS during World War II, specifically in northwest Europe (1944-45). It was a weapon that made use of the hollow-charge anti-armour effect. The PIAT warhead had a circular hollow charge that had a deep impressed cone set into one face of the charge. The idea was to detonate the explosive at a fixed distance from the armour to be penetrated, producing an intense jet of very high temperature particles that would move forward at high speed and burn its way through the armour. In addition, by lining the interior of the explosive cone with a thin layer of metal, the effect could be enhanced (tanks could employ the simple tactic of using stand-off armour – sheets of thin metal attached to their sides – to defeat hollow-charge weapons).

The PIAT had a powerful bomb which could defeat any World War II tank provided the aimer could find the right mark. For example, it could make a hole in the engine compartment of a Tiger but could not penetrate its front armour. It was a reasonably accurate, robust and simple weapon, though rather awkward to cock. To carry out the procedure, the firer placed the shoulder-pad on the ground, held the PIAT upright, stooped down and placed both hands under the trigger-guard. Standing on the pad, he then turned the body of the weapon 90 degrees clockwise and then straightened his back, hauling the gun body up against the spigot spring and thus pulling the spigot back into the body until it clicked onto the sear. Failure to connect resulted in the spring pulling the firer back down with a thud.

The velocity of the bomb was so slow that it could be watched in flight, the firer ducking at the last minute to avoid the lumps of tail and cartridge which often flew back as far as the launch position (there were a number of fatalities during the war because men failed to get their heads down quick enough!).

Weight: 14.51kg (launcher); 1.36kg (grenade)
Length: 990mm
Effective range: 101m
Armour penetration: 110mm

RPG-7 The main man-portable anti-tank weapon of the former Soviet Union, the RPG-7 is in the service of many Third World countries around the globe. Being in such widespread use – it was used by the soldiers of the People's Front for the Liberation of the Occupied Arabian Gulf in Oman, for example – SAS soldiers receive training in its use.

The RPG-7 has been in service since 1962 and, like most Soviet systems, is simple and effective, and in skilled hands it can be put to good use. The latter point is important as the missile has an odd trajectory which drops as it leaves the tube. This means it can hit a piece of

wall or high ground in front of the firer if sufficient clearance has not been allowed. Several IRA terrorists have discovered this tendency to their cost in Northern Ireland. Other 'own goals' with an RPG-7 include an IRA terrorist driving in a van and carrying an RPG-7 by his side. He spotted a British Army armoured personnel carrier (APC) and decided to take a shot at it. Stopping his van at a convenient gap in a hedge, he opened the window and put the rocket launcher to his shoulder and aimed. Lining up a perfect shot he fired the rocket. A split second later the van exploded in a huge fire-ball. The APC was totally unscathed. A subsequent investigation revealed that the terrorist had been transporting around 150kg of home-made explosives in the back of the van which had been ignited by the backflash from the RPG!

Weight: 7.9kg (launcher); 2.25kg (missile)
Length: 950mm
Effective range: 300m (moving targets); 500m (stationary targets)
Armour penetration: 330mm

SMAW The Shoulder-launched Multi-purpose Assault Weapon is a man-portable weapon which has a re-usable launcher and can fire High Explosive Dual Purpose (HEDP) and High Explosive Anti-Armour (HEAA) rockets. The former is designed to defeat earth and timber bunkers, concrete and brick walls and light armoured vehicles. The SMAW is, therefore, a true multi-purpose weapon and one that will endear itself to units such as the SAS. It is a fairly new weapon and, as far as is known, has not been tried in battle. Most certainly it has not been used in combat by the SAS. However, test reports have confirmed SMAW to be a fairly simple weapon which is not too heavy and one which performs well against armour and strongpoints. It will undoubtedly be used by the Regiment in the future.

Calibre: 83mm
Weight: 7.5kg
Length: 825mm
Effective range: 250m (HEDP); 500m (HEAA)
Armour penetration: 600mm

Right: Israeli soldiers in Lebanon, June 1982. The man in the foreground is carrying an RPG-7.

Section 3
SURFACE-TO-AIR MISSILES

In general SAS patrols do not carry hand-held surface-to-air missile (SAM) systems. There are three main reasons for this. First, SAS patrols rarely hold static bases that require air-defence systems. Even when a four-man patrol or larger force does establish a base, it is invariably well camouflaged, and SAS units rarely stay at the same location for more than one night. True to their method of operating, SAS teams move fast and stealthily. Second, by their nature SAS patrols are lightly equipped. Hauling around SAM systems that can weigh around 15kg each, in addition to personal weapons and equipment, would only slow down a patrol. Third, because of the SAS's skill in fieldcraft and camouflage techniques, the use of hand-held SAMs is unnecessary in most circumstances.

Nevertheless, there are occasions when it is prudent for SAS teams to possess SAMs. Fighting a war in desert of arctic conditions, for example, greatly increases the chances of a unit operating behind the lines being spotted and attacked by hostile aircraft. There is little or no cover and any movement during daylight hours carries risks. In addition, just as World War II SAS jeep patrols destroyed Axis aircraft behind the lines in North Africa, so might modern-day patrols want to knock out targets of opportunity with SAMs. During the Falklands War, for example, the SAS fired some six or seven Stinger missiles and accounted for an Argentine Pucara aircraft that was flying over the Goose Green area en route to attack the British forces that had recently landed at San Carlos Water.

Blowpipe A weapon used by both the British and Argentinians in the Falklands War, Blowpipe has now been largely replaced by Javelin. This British system consists of a missile with a high explosive warhead, launching canister and a radio-linked aiming and guidance unit. It is optically guided which means that if the aimer is to successfully engage a target he must see it at a minimum range of 3km. In the Falklands, for example, this was often not possible due to poor visibility which reduced the weapon's overall effectiveness. Being optically guided means that it is used against closing targets, unlike heat-seeking systems which are essentially tail-chasing missiles. Overall Blowpipe has sufficient range and an effective warhead. However, having a sophisticated guidance system means only a skilled operator can work it effectively.

Weight: 11kg (missile)
Length: 1.39m
Maximum range: 3.5km
Maximum speed: Mach 1.6

Javelin Essentially a successor to Blowpipe, this British system is electronically more sophisticated and has a greater range and a night sight. It incorporates a Semi-Automatic Command to Line-Of-Sight (SACLOS) guidance system similar to the ones used in anti-tanks weapons. All the firer has to do is keep the aiming mark on the target, and the guidance system will do the rest. Javelin fires a blast/fragmentation warhead and has a proximity or impact fuze, making it a much more effective weapon than Blowpipe.

Weight: 11.1kg
Length: 1.4m
Maximum range: 4km
Maximum speed: over Mach 1.6

Stinger An American system, Stinger is the successor to Redeye. It has an infrared guidance system so the firer does not have to guide the missile himself. It also incorporates an Identification Friend or Foe (IFF) system for the positive identification of hostile aircraft. The great advantage with Stinger is that it does not require the operator to be highly trained in its use (that said, there were reports from Afghanistan of Mujahedeen soldiers firing Stingers the wrong way round – no military system is entirely foolproof it would seem!).

Above right: The Stinger hand-held SAM system was used by the Mujahedeen in Afghanistan, and was also used by the SAS in the Falklands.
Below right: The Blowpipe anti-aircraft weapon. Over 30,000 missiles have been built to date.

The only recorded use of Stinger by the SAS is during the Falklands War. On the night of 20 May, 60 men of D Squadron, 22 SAS, commanded by Major Cedric Delves and supported by HMS *Ardent* in Grantham Sound, were landed by Sea King helicopters to the north of Darwin to prevent the garrison interfering with the British landings which were to take place early the next day at San Carlos Water. The SAS were heavily armed with GPMGs, mortars, Milans and rifles, and were in possession of at least one Stinger missile launcher. The SAS put up such a ferocious barrage of small-arms, mortar and anti-tank missile fire that the Argentinians, also under fire form *Ardent*'s 4.5-inch gun, were contained in their defensive positions. As a result, they were not able to interfere with the landings at San Carlos, which went ahead undisturbed. On the 21st, while moving back to British positions, D Squadron, in open ground, was spotted by an Argentinian Pucara aircraft. The latter swooped down to rake the SAS with cannon fire. However, the trooper with the Stinger quickly took aim and fired the missile. The latter streaked towards the aircraft and hit it, causing the airframe to explode into a ball of fire before the pilot had chance to eject.

The latest version of the weapon is the Stinger-POST (Passive Optical Seeker Technology), designed for better performance at low altitudes and incorporating greater resistance to infrared countermeasures. In addition, Stinger-POST has a programmable microprocessor inbuilt for future cost-effective upgrades.

The system is also being used for vehicle defence. The US Army is currently testing the 'Avenger' vehicle: a 'Hummer' (high mobility, multi-purpose wheeled vehicle) equipped with four Stingers on a pedestal launch.

Weight: 15.8kg
Length: 698mm
Maximum range: 5km
Maximum speed: Mach 2

Right: Javelin, the successor to Blowpipe. The system is electronically more advanced than the latter, has greater range and is equipped with a night sight. It is also extremely accurate. Such qualities do not come cheap; each missile is estimated to cost around £60,000 (1989 prices).

Section 4
GRENADES AND EXPLOSIVES

A grenade is defined as a small bomb which is thrown by hand. Grenades usually consist of a small charge encased in a thick metal case, the latter being corrugated to ensure an even distribution of the fragments on detonation. Most grenades weigh between 500g and 1kg and have a lethal radius of 10-20m. Their general use is described by Bob Bennett, one of the original members of the SAS in World War II: 'If a building was occupied we used grenades. You threw a couple in, then smashed through the door spraying the room with fire as you went.'

It would be impossible to list all the different types of grenades used by the Special Air Service since 1941. Therefore, only brief details of some of the models can be given. The Regiment has mostly used those grenades which were standard-issue models rather than any 'James Bond'-type articles. After all, the SAS trooper wants to achieve the same effect with a grenade as an infantryman: disable enemy positions and/or kill personnel. In World War II, for example, SAS soldiers could often be seen carrying captured German 'potato mashers'. These were in service from 1915 to 1945 and had a wooden handle, a screw-on canister at one end and a screw-off cap at the other. To operate it the thrower removed the head, inserted the detonator, replaced the head, removed the end cap, pulled the string and threw it. Four seconds later the friction ignitor detonated the charge. The British equivalent was the '36' grenade which had the 'traditional' shape of a grenade, i.e. looked like a green pineapple. It was effective enough, though the fragmentation could be erratic and a soldier needed to take cover after he had thrown it.

In its later campaigns the Regiment was again using standard-issue grenades. In Oman in 1959, for example, SAS troopers were using '80' grenades. These were essentially white phosphorus incendiary grenades that were good in the anti-personnel role.

L2A2 The current standard-issue grenade in service with the British Army. It is actually a copy of the American M26 and comprises a thin metal casing containing a coiled wire liner loaded with explosive. It has good fragmentation and lethality at close ranges, though over greater distances the fragments soon lose their velocity.

Haley & Weller This British firm produces a number of grenades including fragmentation and incendiary. They have silent electric fuzes which don't fizz or crack as the handle flies off and thus does not warn the intended target. Though they are not used by the British Army, they would be ideal for SAS-type clandestine operations and it would be strange indeed if the Regiment had not at least examined their potential for such a role.

GRENADE LAUNCHERS

Since the early 1960s grenade launchers have found increasing favour with infantry and special forces units. Why? Range is a major factor. A grenade launcher can propel a projectile of slightly less effect than a hand grenade over a distance of around 300m. However, there are two main problems with grenade launchers. First, since the grenade is travelling in a straight line it cannot go around cover, unlike a hand-thrown grenade. Second, such is the fuzing problem for grenade launchers that two-thirds of the projectile usually consists of fuze, with only a third being explosive content. This means the results at the target end are not as spectacular as one would expect.

Despite these not inconsiderable factors, grenade launchers are still rated highly. This is because current military thinking takes the view that a fragmenting weapon is better than a point weapon, i.e. one firing a bullet, in many situations. Grenade launchers, for example, are looked upon as being particularly useful if a unit is ambushed as it can lay down a large amount of firepower at short notice. Nevertheless, against a bunker or similar strongpoints grenade

Above right: The British L2A2 hand grenade.
Below right: The Claymore mine, a weapon that has its origins in Nazi Germany.

launchers tend to lack overall punch. In these circumstances a mortar or light anti-tank weapon is much more preferable.

The SAS used grenade launchers during the Pebble Island raid in 1982, and it is in the role of a fragmentation weapon for raiding that the Regiment has a use for these weapons. Against the Argentine aircraft on the airstrip, for example, the M203 came into its own, wreaking havoc and damaging the aircraft beyond repair. They were also used to stop any possible Argentine counterattack against D Squadron's troopers. In built-up areas and against buildings they can also be fired through windows, doors and other entrances. One advantage with modern grenade launchers such as the M203 is that they can be attached to assault rifles, thus making them significant force multipliers.

Automatic grenade launchers The current military fashion is to go for what are in effect machine guns firing 40mm grenades up to a range of 300m. These weapons are now being produced by Singapore, Spain, Germany, China and America. Their firepower cannot be doubted, though they are rather bulky and would not be carried by an SAS unit on a long-range patrol. Nevertheless, for defence of a static base, for example, they would come into their own.

Mark 19 This American weapon is an air-cooled, blowback-type machine gun that can fire a variety of grenades including high explosive anti-personnel, dual purpose anti-personnel and armour-piercing. Mounted on a tripod, the Mark 19 is usually fed from 20- or 50-round ammunition containers.
Calibre: 40mm
Weight: 34kg
Length: 1028mm
Effective range: 1600m
Rate of fire: 325-375 rounds per minute (cyclic)
Muzzle velocity: 240 metres per second

SB 40 LAG Produced by the Spanish firm Santa Barbara, this is a belt-fed automatic grenade launcher which, because of its weight, can be used as a general purpose tactical weapon in the field. This attribute makes it attractive to units such as the SAS. It can also be turret-,

tripod- or pedestal-mounted on wheeled and tracked vehicles, boats and helicopters. An additional feature of this weapon is the ability to shift the feed to the left or right side as desired.
Calibre: 40mm
Weight: 30kg (gun); 22kg (tripod); 10.5kg (cradle mount)
Length: 980mm
Effective range: 1500m
Rate of fire: 200 rounds per minute (cyclic)
Feed: 25- or 50-round linked belt
Muzzle velocity: 240 metres per second

M79 Used by the SAS in Oman during the 1970s, the M79 is a single-shot, break-open, breech-loading weapon which was the first designed to fire fin-stabilised grenades. It is a relatively lightweight, robust and accurate weapon that has the added advantage of having a reasonable recoil. A trained man can put a grenade through a window at a range of around 150m, though for greater ranges it is necessary to know the distance because the round has a very high trajectory. One major disadvantage of the M79 is that it is a dedicated weapon, i.e. the man firing it usually carries nothing else and is therefore defenceless after he fires his grenade until he loads another. Despite this, overall the M79 can be classed as a useful support weapon.
Calibre: 40mm
Weight: 2.72kg (unloaded); 2.95kg (loaded)
Length: 737mm
Effective range: 350m (area targets); 150m (point targets)
Muzzle velocity: 76 metres per second

M203 This was developed to overcome the problem encountered because the M79 grenade launcher was a dedicated weapon. The M203 thus satisfies the requirement for a grenade launcher/rifle package as it can be attached beneath the barrel of a rifle, specifically the M16 (the current M203PI can, according to the manufacturer, be fitted to any assault rifle currently in service). This means more men in a section can carry them and so increases the unit's overall firepower. The M203 is lightweight and can fire a variety of grenades including high explosive, anti-personnel and buckshot. The latter type is particularly appropriate as,

Above: The M79 grenade launcher, a weapon used by the SAS in Oman in the 1970s.

unfortunately, the M203 is difficult to shoot accurately, though against large targets such as stationary aircraft it is effective enough, witness its use by the SAS on Pebble Island during the Falklands campaign. Corporal Davey, D Squadron, 22 SAS, took part in this action and used the M203 against enemy personnel: 'Just off the airstrip we heard Spanish forces, at least four or five, shouting some fifty metres towards the settlement. I opened fire with M203 and put down some sixty rounds in the direction of the voices. Two very pained screams were the only reply.'

Calibre: 40mm
Weight: 1.63kg (loaded)
Length: 380mm
Effective range: 400m
Feed: breech-loading, sliding barrel
Muzzle velocity: 75 metres per second

Above: An M203 grenade launcher with M16 rifle.

Rifle grenades The ability to fire grenades from the muzzle of a standard infantry rifle gives small-sized patrols important additional firepower. In the 1960s the Belgian company MECAR developed a number of grenades that could be fired using conventional ball ammunition (previously they could only be fired using blank rounds). The MECAR system – called the Bullet Trap Universal (BTU) – traps the bullet in the grenade's tail and uses the energy of the round to propel the grenade. Currently the MECAR range of rifle grenades is among the best in the world and can be fired from both 5.56mm and 7.62mm calibre rifles.

The range currently available is quite comprehensive, encompassing as it does grenades for many purposes: anti-armour; blast and fragmentation (for use against light structures, material targets and personnel); dual purpose for defeating armour and attacking personnel; delayed blast and fragmentation, whereby the grenade has a pyrotechnic delay of four seconds which allows it to be launched through light structures and to detonate inside; and smoke and incendiary, whereby the grenade can penetrate enclosures and then detonates to produce a fireball of 6m diameter. In the hands of trained soldiers MECAR grenades – which are very accurate and comfortable to shoot — are formidable weapons.

Another Belgian firm, FN Nouvelle Herstal, produces the FN Bullet-Through rifle grenade. This has one major advantage for SAS-type operations: it is very compact, allowing a soldier to carry several. When required for use the tail of the grenade is extended and placed on the muzzle of the rifle. After leaving the muzzle a spring causes the tail to retract into the body and at the same time the firing pin and detonator are brought into alignment. The Bullet-Through is currently available in several versions: anti-personnel, anti-vehicle, smoke and illuminating. They have no drawbacks as far as is known, although they have not yet been used in combat. All the above grenades, both MECAR and those made by FN, are effective up to a range of around 300m and can also be used safely at a range of only 25m.

EXPLOSIVES

Explosives and demolitions have been associated with the SAS since its creation in the North African desert in 1941; indeed, it was originally conceived of by David Stirling to be a unit that would mount sabotage raids behind enemy lines. The months following the unit's creation saw the vindication of Stirling's idea as small SAS parties hit Axis airfields, destroying parked aircraft with explosive charges and small-arms fire. Forty years later, the SAS was again using explosives to destroy enemy aircraft, this time Argentinian ones on Pebble Island.

There are essentially two types of explosive: low explosives and high explosives. In the former, for example gunpowder, detonation is by burning and the process is relatively slow. In high explosives – the type commonly used by special forces – the charge is set off by an initiator. High explosives must be relatively insensitive to prevent premature detonation and must be resistant to heat and humidity. When they are detonated they burn at hypersonic speeds – 2000-8500m per second – and thus the gases released form shock waves that shear and shatter nearby objects. There are two types of initiator: electrical and non-electrical. Detonation by the latter is via a time fuze connected to a non-electric firing cap (the fuze can be a cord comprising of black powder encased in a fibre wrapping). In electrical firing systems detonation occurs when an electric current is passed through wires in the blasting cap which ignites the charge within the cap and detonates the main explosive charge.

The type of explosive used by special forces is mainly plastic, such as RDX or PETN, both having a plasticizer added for improved stability under various temperatures and resistance to water. Explosives are constantly being refined and updated, especially with regard to requirements for special forces, with the result that new explosives are becoming lighter and more destructive. For example, the American Penetration Augmented Munition (PAM) programme has resulted in a charge being designed that can disable a concrete bridge and other structures using a man-portable charge weighing around 15kg. Previously, some 90kg of C-4 explosive would have been needed. The explosive for the PAM currently consists of aluminized RDX.

Being a unit that specialises in operating behind enemy lines, the SAS obviously trains its soldiers in the use of explosives. Four-man SAS patrols can inflict damage on an enemy out of all proportion to their size by destroying aircraft, vehicles, railway lines, holing ships and boats and disabling power lines and exchanges. The value of explosives expertise was illustrated during World War II. While operating in France in 1944, SAS teams cut enemy railway lines hundreds of times and interrupted the transport of German men and materiel. The method was very simple: a charge would be placed under each track which would be set off by a pressure switch activated by a train passing overhead. As with many aspects of SAS work, the simple way is often the best.

Claymore mine Used extensively by the SAS in Borneo – mainly for ambush operations – the Claymore has its origins in World War II. A German named Schardin devised an anti-tank mine in 1944 which consisted of a round, flat dish filled with explosive with a concave plate of steel on its face. He then turned it on its side and fired it. Incredibly, the plate was blown off and went through the front of a Panther tank at 80m range! After the war the Americans took the idea and swapped the steel plate for steel slugs. A very effective anti-personnel weapon was born.

The Claymore fires around 350 metal balls over a fan-shaped area to a range of 100m, shredding anyone unlucky enough to be in the way. It can be activated manually or electrically fired by command or tripwires. During the Vietnam War, the Viet Cong used to strap them to tall trees surrounding likely helicopter landing zones. When any choppers came in to land, the Viet Cong fired the mines and took out the aircraft.

Lewes bomb Bob Bennett, an SAS World War II veteran, describes the technique for dealing with enemy aircraft in North Africa: 'I was with Paddy [Mayne], and we went for the bombers lying under the cover of the trees. We just walked down the line of aircraft lobbing Lewes bombs onto their wings. When the job was finished, Paddy and I sped out the place...When we halted for a break, the bombers started to go up – it must have been about two hours as we were using time pencils of that duration.'

The Lewes bomb was invented by Lieutenant 'Jock' Lewes in 1941 for destroying parked enemy aircraft. It was extremely simple, consisting of half a kilo of plastic explosive rolled in a mixture of thermite from an incendiary bomb and old engine oil. Detonation was by means of a time pencil and a detonator, the former consisting of different strengths of acid which burnt through a wire connected to the plunger of the detonator. This gave a time delay of anything from 10 minutes to two hours. Lewes bombs were used to great effect by the Regiment in North Africa in 1941-42, when dozens of German and Italian aircraft were destroyed by them.

BOATS AND SHIPS

Though operating from ships and submarines is predominantly the preserve of the Special Boat Squadron, the SAS has, since World War II, employed a wide variety of maritime and amphibious vessels in its operations.

The SAS mainly conducts its operations on land. As such, it may seem surprising that a chapter should be included which discusses ships and smaller vessels. However, since World War II the Regiment has used a variety of vessels to transport its men to their operational area. True to David Stirling's original idea that SAS parties should be able to arrive at their objective by land, sea or air, each of the Regiment's four 'Sabre' Squadrons has a Boat Troop that specialises in all aspects of amphibious warfare. Because the Regiment could be called upon to fight in almost any part of the world – involving anything from transportation by large ships across the open seas to using local vessels along jungle waterways – its soldiers must be adept at handling all types of boats. In Borneo, for example, SAS patrols frequently employed native canoes as transport along the country's inland waterways.

Though aircraft have, for the most part, replaced ships as the means of inserting teams into hostile territory, the Falklands War of 1982 illustrated that the Royal Navy still has a part to play in transporting SAS soldiers.

A flotilla of British Type 22 and 42 destroyers. Though these ships fulfil an anti-submarine and aircraft role, they can also be used to transport special forces units, as in the Falklands.

AIRCRAFT CARRIERS & DESTROYERS

AIRCRAFT CARRIERS

HMS *Hermes* There is only one known example of the SAS using an aircraft carrier: HMS *Hermes* during the 1982 Falklands War. On 5 April the ship left Portsmouth; on board, in addition to its normal complement, was a small party of SAS soldiers, a company of Royal Marines and some Special Boat Squadron (SBS) personnel (more SAS soldiers joined the carrier at Ascension Island).

Hermes in British service was essentially an anti-submarine carrier, having a squadron of Sea King anti-submarine helicopters and a small number of V/STOL (Vertical/Short Take-Off and Landing) aircraft on board. In addition, it could also fulfil the role of commando assault carrier and so could have transported the whole of 3 Commando Brigade to the war zone. In the event, it was decided that *Hermes* would carry the helicopters and the Sea Harriers, and would not transport the Royal Marines. One major disadvantage with V/STOL-type carriers – and this was the case during the Falklands War – is that they do not have the capacity to launch long-range interceptors and generally do not carry airborne early warning aircraft.

The SAS was involved with *Hermes* right up to the landings at San Carlos Water on 21 May. Rear-Admiral John Woodward was the commander of the main group of surface warships during Operation 'Corporate' and was based on the carrier. Part of his task was to 'soften up' Argentinian positions on the Falklands through aerial attack, shore bombardment and the reconnaissance of possible landing sites. The latter was the task of special forces – both SAS and SBS – and for this reason part of G Squadron, 22 SAS, was put under Woodward's command. The SAS team's transport were the Sea King helicopters of 846 Squadron on *Hermes*. The reconnaissance missions conducted by special forces before the landings at San Carlos were directed by Colonel Richard Preston of the Royal Marines, also on board. These began in early May and by the middle of the month men from both G

Squadron and the SBS had been flown in and out of the Falklands.

On the night of 14 May, the carrier steamed to the north of the islands to land an SAS party on Pebble Island, where some Argentinian aircraft were based. Accompanying her were the frigate *Broadsword* (an air defence ship for *Hermes*) and the destroyer *Glamorgan* (which would provide shore bombardment). The three ships encountered heavy seas and strong winds as they made their way to the target and, much worse, *Broadsword* started to drop behind. In fact, her Sea Wolf missile system had become defective (this expensive and sophisticated surface-to-air missile had only entered service in 1979 – despite this, it was to prove its worth in the Falklands, shooting down five Argentinian aircraft). *Hermes* sailed to within 65km of land to give her Sea King helicopters a shorter journey to Pebble Island in the strong wind. The aircraft took off carrying the troopers from D Squadron. Five hours later they returned, the SAS having destroyed the aircraft in an extremely successful operation. The carrier and *Glamorgan* then headed east at speed back to the other ships in the Task Force, not wanting to be caught by enemy submarines or aircraft.

On 19 May, men and equipment were being redistributed among the ships of the Task Force to prepare for the amphibious landings and to ensure that if a ship was sunk it would not result in an inordinate loss of life. This was particularly true of the liner *Canberra* which had sailed from Southampton with nearly 3000 men on board (40 Commando, 42 Commando and 3 Para). These plans also included the special forces and the Sea Kings on board *Hermes*. Fortunately the weather was calm on the day and the transfers went ahead fairly smoothly. In one of the last flights of the day, Sea King helicopter number ZA 294 carrying three crew and 27 passengers was approaching HMS *Intrepid* when it crashed into the sea. The cause of the accident has never

Above right: *Hermes*' replacement, HMS *Illustrious*.
Below right: The frigate HMS *Brilliant*.

been fully established, though the explanation of it being the combination of an overloaded helicopter and a tired crew seems the most plausible. Whatever the reason, 21 men, 18 of them soldiers from D Squadron, died.

The SAS's involvement with *Hermes*, however, had not entirely ceased. After the landings at San Carlos (21 May), both *Hermes* and *Invincible* moved closer to the islands to allow their Sea Harriers to conduct missions over the land theatre of operations. A four-man SAS team from G Squadron led by Captain Aldwin Wight had established a covert observation post near the islands' capital, Stanley. They had discovered that the Argentinians moved their helicopters to a dispersal area some 16km west of the town each night. The SAS relayed this information back to *Hermes* which despatched two Harriers to attack the site. This was promptly carried out, a Chinook and two Pumas being destroyed by the aircrafts' cannons.

Hermes returned intact from the Falklands and was sold to the Indian Navy three years later. She is still in service today, named *Viraat*.

Type: multi-role aircraft carrier
Displacement: 28,700 tons (fully loaded)
Aircraft: six Sea Harrier fighters and seven Sea King helicopters. A maximum of 37 aircraft can be carried
Performance: maximum speed 28kt
Complement: 1350 including air group
Armament: two quadruple Sea Cat SAM launchers (Sea Cat is a short-range system which, because of its low speed and limited range, is largely ineffective against high-performance aircraft and anti-ship missiles)

DESTROYERS

Like aircraft carriers, the Falklands War is the only time the SAS has been involved with Royal Navy destroyers to any great extent. These warships are not designed for the transportation of troops, being fast, unarmoured, heavily armed warships that are intended – at least in the British Navy – to be anti-air and anti-submarine warfare vessels armed with long-range surface-to-air missiles, depth charges and helicopters. However, as often happens in war, the Royal Navy was called upon to employ its ships in varying roles during the Falklands campaign. The transporting of special forces to the war zone was one of these missions.

HMS *Antrim* This 'County' class ship was one of the first purpose-built guided-missile destroyers. In fact, *Antrim* was one of the more modern of the 'County' class, being equipped with Exocet anti-ship missiles and the Mk 2 Seaslug surface-to-air missile.

Antrim's involvement with the SAS is really the story of the taking of South Georgia and the remarkable exploits of its Wessex helicopter. On 7 April 1982, *Antrim*, the frigate *Plymouth* and the fleet tanker *Tidespring* were detached from the main Task Force sailing from Gibraltar and were detailed to retake the island of South Georgia prior to the main assault on the Falklands themselves. The small group of ships were given the designation Task Force 319.9 and were led by *Antrim*'s commander, Captain B.C. Young. At Ascension Island the flotilla was joined by the fleet auxiliary *Fort Austin* carrying D Squadron, 22 SAS, the latter having been flown to the island. In addition, there were some SBS soldiers with the group and M Company, 42 Commando (nicknamed the 'Mighty Munch').

An operations room was established onboard *Antrim* to determine the best way of taking the island. It was decided that D Squadron's Mountain Troop would be landed on Fortuna Glacier and then move south and establish observation posts around the main Argentinian positions at Leith and Grytviken. On 21 April, the troop was landed on the glacier by the Wessex from *Antrim* and the two from *Tidespring*. The mission was a complete disaster, the weather closed in quickly, forcing the commander of the party, Captain John Hamilton, to request evacuation the next day to prevent his men getting frostbite and hypothermia (the men spent a thoroughly wretched night in one small tent and bivvy bags).

On 22 April, the helicopters returned to extract the men. They landed and picked up the troop. However, once airborne one Wessex hit a 'whiteout' and crashed. The other two aircraft landed and picked up the disabled helicopter's crew and its passengers (fortunately no one had been killed). Then one of the surviving aircraft

Right: The carrier *Hermes*. During the Falklands War her Sea King helicopters took part in the highly successful Pebble Island raid.

also encountered severe weather and crashed. This left only one Wessex, the one piloted by Lieutenant-Commander Ian Stanley from *Antrim*. He flew his passengers back to the ship and then returned carrying blankets, medical assistance and supplies. However, he could not land owing to the poor weather conditions and was forced to return to his ship. Returning again, a gap in the weather allowed him to land and pick up the men. Stanley deservedly won the Distinguished Service Order for his flying skills and bravery that day.

On 23 April, D Squadron's Boat Troop attempted to establish positions on Grass Island using Gemini boats. However, two of the craft broke down and were swept away by heavy winds. Although one managed to land on South Georgia, the other was in danger of being lost in

the ocean before being found by the redoubtable Wessex from *Antrim*.

News from London that an Argentinian submarine was approaching the force scattered the British ships. However, two days later, on 25 April, it reassembled to conduct a daring attack on Grytviken (apart from *Tidespring* which was well out to sea). *Antrim*, *Plymouth* and the frigate *Brilliant* (which had reached the area the day before) steamed towards the settlement. The Argentinian submarine *Santa Fe* had been disabled by a helicopter attack and was stranded in the harbour, and so it was decided to attack the Argentinians before M Company, in *Tidespring*, came up. The commander of the land assault, Major Guy Sheridan, therefore put together three troops for a heliborne assault on Grytviken: one of Royal Marines, one of SBS men, and the third made up of SAS troopers.

The men were put ashore while *Antrim* and *Plymouth* pounded the shore with their 4.5-inch guns – though they were under specific orders from London not to damage the buildings. After landing the men moved forward and approached the enemy positions. A radio signal was sent to the ships requesting they steam into the bay and level the buildings if the Argentinians refused to surrender. *Antrim* did so and the enemy hoisted a white flag. The SAS and Royal Marines had not fired a shot.

After the taking of South Georgia, *Antrim* and the SAS troopers went on to join the main Task Force to take part in the rest of the campaign. On 21 May she was damaged by an air attack but suffered no fatalities.

Type: guided-missile destroyer
Displacement: 6800 tons (fully loaded)
Aircraft: one Wessex helicopter
Performance: maximum speed 32kt
Complement: 472
Armament: four single Exocet launchers; one twin Seaslug SAM launcher; one twin 114mm dual purpose gun; two quadruple Sea Cat SAM launchers; and two single 20mm anti-aircraft guns

Left: HMS *Hermes* returning to Portsmouth after her participation in the Falklands campaign. Before the British landings at San Carlos Water, the carrier was used to fly SAS and SBS teams in and out of the islands by helicopter.

Section 2
TRANSPORT AND ASSAULT SHIPS

During World War II, specifically the campaigns in Sicily and Italy in 1943, and the Falklands War of 1982, the SAS made use of a host of transport and assault vessels. In the latter conflict, for example, the Regiment employed the Royal Fleet Auxiliary ships *Resource* and *Fort Austin* to transport men to the combat zone. The former was used to ship men from G Squadron to the theatre of operations and the latter was used to take D Squadron to South Georgia (Mountain Troop of the squadron was later moved onto the ice-patrol ship *Endurance* and then HMS *Antrim*).

The 'Fort' class of fleet replenishment ships have four holds, each capable of storing 3500 tons of palletized munitions, provisions and stores. To handle this load each ship has three 10-ton and three five-ton capacity cranes, in addition to sliding-stay constant-tension transfer rigs on each side in order to carry out alongside replenishment operations. The ships can carry up to four anti-submarine warfare (ASW) helicopters which means they can act as a floating base for a task group's ASW force.

During the Falklands, campaign the SAS also made use of the 'Fearless' class assault support ship *Intrepid*. On 19 May, the transfer of the special forces organisation from *Hermes* to *Intrepid* took place. Tragically, in one of the last helicopter flights of the day, a Sea King crashed into the ocean, killing 18 men from D Squadron.

The 'Fearless' class of ships provide amphibious assault capabilities by means of an onboard naval assault group/brigade headquarters unit with a fully equipped operations room. From here a force commander can mount and control all sea, air and land aspects of the operation. Like all ships of its class, *Intrepid* has a floodable well deck that allows landing craft and hovercraft to load or discharge troops. Access is via a large folding door in the stern. In addition, a platform over the well serves as a landing pad for helicopters or Harrier aircraft. There are three vehicle decks: one for tracked vehicles (tanks or self-propelled guns), one for wheeled trucks, and a half-deck for Land Rovers and trailers.

Another type of assault ship used by the Regiment in the Falklands was the 'Sir Lancelot' and 'Sir Bedivere' class of landing ships. A small party of SAS men were on board *Sir Galahad* at Fitzroy when it was attacked by Argentinian Dagger and Skyhawk aircraft. The resulting bomb explosions that rocked the ship claimed the lives of 45 men, mostly Welsh Guardsmen caught in the open vehicle and tank deck, and inflicted injuries on a further 150. The SAS troopers, because they were stationed near the bow of the ship, got away with light injuries. This type of ship is fitted with ramps and doors in the bow and stern to allow vehicles to board and leave. There is also a helicopter landing pad at the stern and a helipad on the foredeck.

During World War II, the SAS had to make do with vessels that had not been originally designed for amphibious warfare. This was particularly true of the campaigns to liberate Sicily and Italy respectively. Prior to the assault on Capo Murro di Porco on 10 July 1943, for example, the men of the Special Raiding Squadron (1 SAS renamed) were transported to the area in the ex-ferry *Ulster Monarch*, it was only when they had to make the actual beach landing that they were transferred to Landing Craft Assault (LCA) boats.

During the Sicilian and Italian campaigns in particular, the SRS and 2 SAS worked closely with the Royal Navy, the latter often having to ferry the men ashore in landing craft. The relationship was not always a happy one, however. During Operation 'Baytown' in September 1943, for example, the SRS was detailed to capture Bagnara on the Italian mainland to support the Allied invasion. The Royal Navy transported the soldiers in Landing Craft Infantry (LCI) vessels. The force left Catania on 1 September 1943. However, almost immediately the craft encountered difficulties: one vessel got a cable caught around its propeller

Above right: A World War II Landing Craft, Tank. Such vessels were used by the SAS in 1943.
Below right: The assault ship *Intrepid*.

and the other ran aground, though it was subsequently refloated. Two days later they reached Allassio, only for one to again run aground. Eventually the SRS was forced to transfer to four smaller LCAs.

The LCI was a relatively fast vessel designed to carry approximately 210 troops on sea crossings lasting anything up to 48 hours. They were use by the SRS again in early October to capture the port of Termoli on the Italian mainland. Along with two Commandos, the 207-strong SRS approached the town in one LCI. Amazingly, the same thing happened that occurred at Bagnara: the vessel ran aground.

Again the men had to be ferried ashore in the much smaller LCAs.

LCAs were used by 2 SAS during its attack on Italian positions on the southeast coast of Sicily on 10 July 1943 (Operation 'Narcissus'). These craft were once described by a man who worked in them as 'like floating bootboxes pretending to be motorboats, mere square shells for carrying troops'. The conditions inside a LCA could be extremely grim: the troops along both sides were covered from the worst of the elements, however those who sat on the centreline row had to put up with constant spray which hastened the onslaught of sea sickness.

Complement: 185 plus 36 crew
Armament: two single 20mm anti-aircraft guns

HMS *Intrepid*
Type: landing platform dock
Displacement: 12,210 tons (fully loaded)
Aircraft: five Wessex or four Sea King plus three Gazelle or Lynx helicopters
Performance: 21kt
Complement: 617
Troops: 330 normal, 670 maximum
Cargo: 20 main battle tanks, one beach armoured recovery vehicle, 45 four-ton trucks or up to 2100 tons of stores, four Landing Craft Utility (LCU), four Landing Craft, Vehicles and Personnel (LCVP), plus helicopters
Armament: four quadruple Sea Cat SAM launchers and two 40mm anti-aircraft guns

RFA *Sir Galahad*
Type: landing ship logistic
Displacement: 5674 tons (fully loaded)
Aircraft: three Wessex or two Sea King or three Gazelle or Lynx helicopters
Performance: 17kt
Complement: 69
Cargo: 18 main battle tanks, 32 four-ton trucks, 120 tons of petrol, oil and lubricants, 30 tons of ammunition, two Mexeflottes, plus helicopters
Armament: two 40mm anti-aircraft guns

Landing Craft, Infantry
Displacement: 384 tons (fully loaded)
Performance: 14kt
Range: 14,822km
Complement: 29
Capacity: 210 troops
Armament: five single 20mm anti-aircraft guns

Landing Craft, Assault
Displacement: 13 tons (fully loaded)
Performance: 7kt
Range: 150km
Complement: four
Capacity: 35 troops

These mass-produced vessels were slow in open seas unless a tow was available, and were vulnerable to enemy fire. The LCA was steered from a position sited forward on the starboard side. The troops exited via armoured doors at the bow which protected them from head-on fire while the boat was approaching the beach.

RFA *Fort Austin*
Type: fleet replenishment ship
Displacement: 22,749 tons (fully loaded)
Aircraft: between one and four Westland Sea King or Wessex helicopters
Performance: 22kt

Section 3
SUBMARINES

Though actual SAS wartime experience with submarines is limited, being restricted to World War II, there are some very good reasons why the submarine is ideally suited to special forces missions. First, its ability to approach a hostile shore underwater means SAS teams can make clandestine landings. Second, it is a much safer method of transporting troops to the theatre of operations than by slow-moving, vulnerable troop ships. In addition, the latter require escort vessels and air cover, if available, whereas a submarine has less chance of being detected. Of course a submarine does not have the space to accommodate a large number of troops. However, as David Stirling originally envisaged small-sized SAS teams hitting individual targets, and the Regiment today mostly operates with four-man squads or 16-man troops, this is not such a problem.

In early 1943, several SAS teams operating in the Mediterranean were transported to their targets by submarine. On 28 May 1943, a party from 2 SAS was dropped off the island of Pantelleria to carry out a detailed reconnaissance of the place. Making their way to the shore by rubber dinghy, they only managed to capture one guard before returning to the submarine. Operation 'Marigold' was a joint SAS/SBS mission to Sardinia, again by submarine, to carry out reconnaissance of enemy airfields on the east coast. However, as soon as they landed the men encountered a hail of gunfire from the enemy, forcing them to beat a hasty retreat.

Interestingly, because of their slow underwater speeds, World War II submarines were really 'submersibles', i.e. vessels that could submerge briefly to approach targets or evade pursuit. They therefore had boat-like hulls designed for high surface speeds and, in addition, often mounted heavy deck guns that reduced underwater performance even further. Submarines tended to attack at night, on the surface and at close range, firing unguided 'straight-running' torpedoes.

Modern British submarines are of two types: diesel-electric and nuclear. The former rely on battery-powered electric motors for underwater propulsion, while diesel engines provide the power for surface movement. Their one major drawback is that they can only operate at high speeds underwater for short periods – usually only a few hours. Once the batteries are discharged the ship must return to the surface to recharge them. While on the surface the vessel is very vulnerable to attack from aircraft or other ships (though modern submarines have retractable snorkels that supply air to the diesel engines while the submarine is submerged, the vessel is still at risk from attack as it is only some 20m below the surface while carrying out the procedure). Nuclear-powered submarines, on the other hand, are capable of sustained submerged speeds and endurance.

'S' Class
Type: World War II British submarine
Displacement: 860 tons
Performance: 16kt (surface); 9kt (underwater)
Complement: 44
Armament: one 101mm gun and six 533mm torpedo tubes
Range: 13,897km

'Upholder' Class
Type: patrol/attack submarine currently in service
Displacement: 2160 tons
Performance: 12kt(surface); 20kt (underwater)
Complement: 44
Armament: 18 Spearfish and Tigerfish torpedoes, four Sub-Harpoon anti-ship missiles
Range: 14,805km

'Trafalgar' Class
Type: nuclear-powered attack submarine
Displacement: 4700 tons
Performance: 20kt (surface); 32kt (underwater)
Complement: 97
Armament: 25 Spearfish and Tigerfish torpedoes, five Sub-Harpoon anti-ship missiles

Above right: The nuclear-powered HMS *Superb*.
Below right: The diesel submarine *Onslaught*.

Section 4
LIGHT ASSAULT CRAFT

Folbot A two-man collapsible sports canoe used by the SAS occasionally in World War II. In March 1942, for example, David Stirling, the Regiment's founder, and a small party of men drove into enemy-held Benghazi to attack shipping moored in the harbour. However, they discovered the folbot had been damaged during the journey and, in addition, the water was too choppy. They were thus forced to retire, having achieved nothing.

The folbot had a wooden frame within a rubberized canvas cover. Although it was theoretically collapsible, in practice it was usually kept fully assembled, all the joints bound up by heavy black insulation tape to prevent accidental disconnection. The folbot was 1.52m long and had rudder lines running to each paddler position. One major drawback with this canoe was that it was too lightly built to pull across mud flats when fully loaded.

Infantry Recce Boat This had a black rubber skin and was inflated by means of a hand pump. Capable of carrying six men, it was not very manoeuvrable in windy conditions. Two were used by the SAS in mid-May 1942, when David Stirling entered the enemy-held port of Benghazi to sabotage shipping there. This was the second attempt by Stirling to destroy enemy transports but, like the first, he was to be frustrated because both boats were defective. Eventually the party was forced to leave Benghazi empty handed. The boat when inflated was 2.6m long and weighed 28kg, though when folded it could be fitted into a canvas bag 1.1m x 560mm x 230mm.

Gemini These craft were used by the SAS during the operation to retake South Georgia in 1982 (see above). Their powerplant can be either an 18-horsepower or 40-horsepower outboard engine and they come in three sizes: a 12-man version 5.2m long, a 10-man version 3.8m long, and an eight-man version 1.6m long.

Klepper canoe Originally introduced into service in the 1950s and still in use today, the Klepper is a German two-man collapsible sports canoe constructed of ash and birch and covered with a deck of cotton woven with hemp and a hull of rubber with a core of polyester cord. The skin is loose-fitting over the frame until the airsponsons under each gunwale are inflated. The Klepper is 5.2m long and 890mm wide.

Motor Torpedo Boats In World War II, between the end of the campaign in North Africa and the invasion of Sicily, the SAS conducted a number of raids against enemy-held islands in the Mediterranean. Though submarines were often used for transport, Royal Navy motor torpedo boats were also employed for the same task, such as in May 1943, when a party from 2 SAS was taken to the island of Lampedusa to destroy a radar station there. The following specifications relate to the MTB 102.
Performance: 40kt
Armament: two 533mm torpedoes and combinations of 20mm cannon, and machine guns

Rigid Raider These fast craft are currently in service with the SAS. Powered by a high-performance 140-horsepower outboard engine, they are ideal for delivering a small team at high speed onto a hostile shore. Capable of carrying eight passengers, Rigid Raiders were widely used by both the SAS and SBS in the Falklands for picking up patrols, re-supply and insertion.

Subskimmer This vessel can operate as a high-speed surface vessel or as a submersible, being able to switch between the two roles as and when required. In addition, it is possible to approach a target in 'snorkel' mode, where only the air inlet, exhaust pipes and the divers' heads are visible. The craft may also be 'parked' on the seabed and left while the divers complete their mission. On the surface the subskimmer is powered by one 90-horsepower engine, while underwater propulsion is by two 24v electric engines.

Above right: Rigid Raiders on the shoreline.
Below right: A Gemini photographed at speed.

COMMUNICATIONS

A prime duty of the SAS is to report back from behind enemy lines. In this role, reliable and robust communications equipment is essential. Since World War II, SAS teams have used a wide range of communications equipment.

I n wartime SAS teams are expected to infiltrate behind enemy lines and establish covert observation posts (OPs) to gather information regarding the movements and dispositions of the opponent's forces. This intelligence is then relayed back to friendly headquarters where it can be used to create an accurate picture of the enemy's strength. Clearly, good communications equipment is essential for the timely transmission of this intelligence, though the kit used by units such as the SAS must also be rugged and secure, i.e. transmit messages in difficult conditions without revealing the location of the operator to the enemy.

Before looking at the types of radio sets that have been used by the SAS since 1941 and the equipment that is currently used by the Regiment, it would be useful to provide an 'idiot's guide' to the workings of military radio systems. At the centre of all radio communications lies the electromagnetic spectrum – the frequency range of electromagnetic radiation from zero through to infinity. All matter emits, reflects and absorbs electromagnetic radiation, the frequency of the radiation being directly proportional to its energy state (electromagnetic radiation is measured and classified both by its wavelength – expressed in metres – and

A simulation of a patrol using the Magellan GPS system. Used by the SAS in the Gulf War, communication between ground troops and satellites has greatly aided accurate military navigation.

by its frequency of oscillation – expressed in Hertz, one Hertz being one cycle per second; as the wavelength becomes longer, the frequency lessens and vice versa). The spectrum is divided into 'regions' ranging from the lowest to the highest frequencies: radio-frequency, infrared, visible light, ultraviolet, x-rays and gamma rays.

The radio-frequency region, which is used for radio communications, radar and navigation aids, is subdivided into frequency bands:

Extra Low Frequency (ELF) – the low frequency, long-wavelength of the spectrum, having a frequency of 300Hz to 3KHz and a wavelength of 1000-100km. This band is used for submarine communications.

Very Low Frequency (VLF) – 3-30KHz and a wavelength of 100-10km. Again, mainly used for submarine communications.

Low Frequency (LF) – between 30 and 300Khz (10-1km). Used mainly for civilian 'long wave' radio channels.

Medium Frequency (MF) – lies between 300KHz and 3MHz (1km-100m) and is used for civilian 'medium wave' radio channels.

High Frequency (HF) – lies between 3 and 30MHz (100-10m). HF signals can travel by both a ground wave and a sky wave. In the latter the signals bounce off the ionosphere (a region of ionized layers that reflects radio waves) and then bounce back to earth, then bounce back to the ionosphere, and so on around the world. The signals can be received whenever they return the earth. Widely used by civilian 'short wave' radio stations, HF bands are too crowded and jammable for military use.

Very High Frequency (VHF) – lies between 30 and 300MHz (10-1m) and is used for television, civilian local radio stations and military tactical radios at the lower command levels. Limited to short ranges, it has a wider band of frequencies than HF though again tends to be very crowded. A major disadvantage of VHF for military use is that it can be intercepted across the whole range of its frequencies and jammed by the enemy.

Ultra High Frequency (UHF) – this band, which lies between 300MHz and 3GHz (1m-10cm), has a greater power requirement but also has a narrower, more dedicated – thus less jammable – beam. Its range can be increased by bouncing the signal off the troposphere (the lowest atmospheric layer) in a phenomenon known as 'tropospheric scatter'.

Super High Frequency (SHF) – has a band of 3-30GHz (10-1cm). Also known as the 'microwave' or 'centrimetric band', it is used for satellite radio communications and radar. Though the majority of combat radios operate in the VHF and UHF bands, these frequencies are now very crowded and so microwave radio is becoming increasingly popular for military transmissions as it is largely unjammable. It relies on a fine beam that needs a clear, unobstructed line of sight and, because it has a very high operational range, it is perfect for satellite-relayed transmissions. The only drawback is that the antenna has to be set up in the right direction which can preclude its use by mobile units.

Extremely High Frequency (EHF) – lies between 30 and 300GHz (1cm-1mm). Called the 'millimetric band', it has two drawbacks: its transmissions cannot be carried by conventional cable, and at long ranges many of its bands are weakened by the atmosphere.

Though communications are essential for modern military operations, there are two main disadvantages with radio and satellite transmissions. First, they can usually be intercepted by the enemy. Electronic signal monitoring (ESM) systems are based on broad-band radio-frequency receivers that are tuned into the wavelengths of an opponent's emitters. The systems are backed up by powerful signal processors and computer banks containing all known emitter characteristics. Thus ESM systems, using direction-finding equipment, can usually quickly identify and locate the source of radio signals. Second, radio is vulnerable to

Above right: The S-Phone, as used by the SAS.
Below right: The bulky No 11 wireless set.

electronic countermeasures (ECM), especially jamming and deception by, for example, drowning a signal using high-power continuous wave transmissions.

Security measures can be incorporated into radio systems to reduce the risk of their being intercepted or jammed by the enemy. Encryption devices make it very difficult for the enemy to decipher what is being said. However, encryption devices take up greater bandwidth (the frequency band taken up by a user) than a non-secure system. 'Frequency hopping' is another method to prevent interception by the enemy. This means the radio automatically changes frequency many times a second in a pattern that is only known to the receiver and transmitter, and so appear random to any other listener. However, the system is not foolproof because, like any other code, they can be eventually deciphered. In addition, 'hopping' takes up a lot of frequencies.

Finally, a word about transmission of data. Voice is the most common method of sending a message by radio. However, it has two disadvantages for the transmission of large amounts of data: there is a very real possibility of misunderstandings, and the longer a radio transmits the greater the chance of its detection by the enemy. One way round these problems is to use a data entry device. Approximately computer keyboard size, it consists of a keyboard, a display screen, a data store and a connection to a radio. The data to be transmitted is first fed into the device, which is not connected to the radio. When the operator is ready he connects the device to the radio and sends the transmission in 'burst' form which is much faster than by voice (Morse code, used by the SAS, can also be sent by this method).

WORLD WAR II

Many of the radio sets used by the SAS during World War II, especially up to 1944, were very large and heavy. The traditional image of lightly armed and equipped teams on foot behind enemy lines is negated somewhat when one considers that the radio set could weigh up to 30kg (it was customary, and still is, for the batteries to be distributed around the unit to alleviate the load carried by the signaller).

No 11 Set In service between 1935 and 1945, this was a very large, bulky system which was totally unsuited to SAS operations on foot. Though it could be mounted on vehicles, the transceiver alone weighed 26kg. In addition, its range was rather poor, only being able to transmit up to 19km with a three-metre aerial.

No 22 Set Used by the SAS in North Africa and the Mediterranean between 1941 and 1943, this was another large, heavy radio set The sender/receiver unit weighed 16.5kg and the power unit 9kg. The No 22 set had a range of around 16km. The SAS soldiers who were landed on Crete to attack enemy airfields, for example, were issued with these radios, as were the SBS men who accompanied them.

S-Phone and Eureka beacon Clandestine missions behind enemy lines require communications equipment that is lightweight, compact and secure, i.e. everything that sets such as the No 11 and 22 weren't. The equipment needs to be able to link up with supply aircraft that are dropping men and materiel to the ground party. In addition, by using a narrow emission beam and ultrashort waves, the equipment can operate securely, with little chance of detection. One major problem remains: the navigator of the aircraft has to locate his tiny target, often at night and at a low altitude, with fog an ever-present threat. A way round this is to miniaturize a radio beacon which can guide the aircraft down a narrow corridor and indicate exactly where the supplies are to be dropped.

During World War II, the SAS used the S-Phone and the Eureka beacon to fulfil these tasks. The S-Phone was really a radiotelephone, homing beacon and parachute dropping indicator all in one. Stored in an aluminium box 500mm long, 200mm wide and 100mm deep, its total weight was 6kg including belt and batteries. After the D-Day landings, when SAS parties were parachuted behind enemy lines and established numerous bases throughout France, S-Phones were continually used to administer the dropping of supplies, though they could also be used between a ship and the shore. The S-Phone had an average range of 20km for an aircraft flying at an altitude of 150m. This increased to 100km at an altitude of 3050m. However, radiotelephone contact could not be established with an aircraft until it was between two and 15 minutes from its arrival time overhead.

The Eureka beacon was a portable radar responder that acted as a homing beacon and a parachute drop indicator, but could not be used as a radiotelephone. As well as being used by the SAS, the Eureka beacon did valuable work for the RAF. British agents operating in France established a number of Eurekas with telescopic aerials in specific geographical locations – mostly in barns or sheds. They were started at nightfall and shut off every morning, and they acted as a secret homing device chain for RAF bombers hitting targets in Europe using routes that were well away from anti-aircraft zones.

A typical drop in France, undertaken countless times in the weeks and months following D-Day, would be as follows: an open field approximately 900m long would be chosen and three red lights placed 100m apart in the middle of the field. A fourth light, a white one, would be placed approximately 45m to the right of the last red light, so the lights were in an L-shaped formation. The white light flashed Morse recognition letters when the aircraft arrived overhead. The latter approached at an altitude of between 150 and 200m, as slowly as possible, and dropped its canisters when it was over the second red light. In France, the SAS were often accompanied and helped by members of the French Resistance to administer drops and unload containers. In some cases fires were set to act as the three red beacons, with car lamps substituting for the white light.

Because the sets were powered by batteries, several types of battery rechargers were developed by the British. These included the wind recharger which consisted of a small windmill mounted on a collapsible three metre-high pole. However, one of the most remarkable was the steam recharger which consisted of a boiler suspended over a brazier and attached to a small two-cylinder steam engine, the latter being coupled to a generator. When working the steam pressure could be used to charge a six-volt battery.

Above: British Paras in action in the Radfan. The soldier in the foreground is using an A41 set.

MCR 1 Known as the 'biscuit receiver', this was designed during the second half of World War II. It was a full-range, highly sensitive receiver which had five miniature tubes. The receiver was contained in a Huntley & Palmer biscuit tin, hence the name, and had two or three batteries – each one being able to provide around 30 hours of reception time. The MCR 1 came with four interchangeable coil units that were plugged onto the pins at the end of the receiver, each unit covering different frequencies. Used by the SAS in northwest Europe (1944-45), some 10,000 'biscuit receivers' were built, over half of them being used for clandestine operations.

POST-WORLD WAR II

SARBE Used by the SAS from the mid-1950s onwards, the SARBE beacon is a lightweight radio beacon which enables ground patrols to link up with supporting aircraft. The unit's battery gives a beacon life of 75 hours, though this is reduced if the voice facility is used a lot. Its range depends on the type of country it is operating in and the altitude of the aircraft. It has an average range of 95km to an aircraft at an altitude of 3000m, and 8-24km to an aircraft flying at an altitude of 300m. The voice facility can contact an aircraft 8km away at an altitude of 300m. The whole unit weighs 1.45kg.

A41 First introduced into service in 1960, this was the standard British Army tactical radio set until 1978. As such, it was used by the Regiment in Aden (1964-67), Borneo (1963-66) and Oman (1970-76). Usually carried in a backpack, the A41 weighed nearly 5kg excluding the battery.

PRC320 This system is part of the British Army's Clansman range of radio equipment for use by combat troops in any environment in the world. It is particularly suited for use with special forces because of its sky-wave facility and hand generator system. Features include a choice of 280,000 frequencies, sky-wave communications at ranges from 50-2000km, and a ground-wave range of over 40km.

   The system is worn on the operator's back, allowing him the use of both arms to wield a weapon. It is powered by rechargeable nickel-cadmium batteries – which have an operating life of 12 hours – or the radio can be powered by a hand-generator system. In addition, it can be remotely operated up to a distance of 3km. The radio operates in the 2-30MHz range and is capable of working in all extremes of weather. The unit itself is 102mm high and weighs 5.6kg.

PRC319 The radio set currently in use with the SAS, the PRC319 is a microprocessor-based tactical radio which gives up to five times more transmission power per kilogram weight than any other portable military radio. It consists of four detachable units: a transmitter/receiver, electronic message unit and two antenna tuners. It has an integral pocket-size electronic message unit which weighs 0.7kg and is removable from the radio for independent operation. It is powered by a small internal battery and is capable of storing messages for up to 500 hours. The PRC319 can store up to 20 pre-set channels in its electronic memory. The unit has a frequency range of 1.5-40MHz and can transmit messages in burst mode. Thus messages are

Above: A British Pathfinder using a PRC319.

loaded via a keyboard, displayed and checked, and then sent in a single burst by pressing a key. The transmission can also be encrypted, making it extremely difficult for the message to be decoded.

Global Positioning System The American-developed Global Positioning System (GPS) was used operationally for the first time during the 1991 Gulf War against Iraq. Among its users was Britain's Special Air Service Regiment.

   GPS consists of a number of satellites positioned above the earth – each one orbits the globe twice a day – which transmit precise time and position (latitude, longitude and altitude) information on a 24-hour basis. Using a GPS receiver users can determine their location anywhere on earth. The system is set to go fully operational in 1993, by which time there will be 21 satellites and three spares orbiting the earth providing 24-hour two- and three-dimensional positioning to any user anywhere on earth.

   How does it work? The whole system is based on precise time and position information. Each satellite, using atomic clocks (accurate to

Above: The Magellan GPS NAV 1000M receiver.

within one second every 300,000 years) and location data, continuously broadcasts the time and its position. A GPS receiver, listening to three or more satellites at once, picks up these signals to determine the user's position on earth. The receiver, by measuring the time interval between the transmission and the reception of a satellite signal, calculates the distance between the user and each satellite. It then calculates the position of the user by utilizing the distance measurements of at least three satellites – four in the case of a three-dimensional (latitude, longitude and altitude) positioning – in an algorithm computation. The position information on a receiver can be displayed in various ways according to user requirements. For example, military users can have the information shown as Military Grid coordinates.

Each satellite continuously broadcasts two signals: a commercial Standard Positioning Service (SPS) signal for civilian users, and a Precise Positioning Service (PPS) signal for military use. The Magellan GPS NAV 1000M military receiver was the system used by United Nations forces during Operation 'Desert Storm' (though only 14 satellites were operational at the time). It is a Small Lightweight GPS Receiver (SLGR) that weighs 0.85kg with batteries and measures 210mm x 90mm x 50mm. Constructed of high-impact, thermal-formed plastic and high-impact-absorbing thermal plastic rubber, it is waterproof, can withstand extremes of temperatures, and its liquid crystal display can run continuously for up to seven hours.

Its application in Saudi Arabia, Kuwait and Iraq quickly became apparent. In a poorly mapped terrain characterised by featureless landscape where sandstorms could reduce visibility to zero, hand-held GPS receivers gave troops constant read-outs of their exact location. For small-sized teams operating behind enemy lines, such as the SAS, GPS receivers enabled them to move quickly and accurately through the barren terrain, at night if need be. GPS units were also used for other tasks: search and rescue, deployment/extraction of troops, intelligence gathering, fire direction, ground troop navigation, obtaining fixes on enemy troop positions, and precise targeting for 'smart' weapons.

A total of 400 GPS receivers were issued to British troops during the course of the war and many of them were used by SAS troopers. One of their great advantages was that they could be used to set up a rendezvous point in the desert to enable SAS teams to re-arm and refuel. Thus a unit could request re-supply, select a waypoint along its route and arrive at the location to find the supplies waiting to be picked up. In addition, each receiver can store position coordinates so the unit can make a return trip if necessary. When the enemy was located, the receiver's targeting calculation function allowed immediate identification and marking of these locations by determining their position grid coordinates. These functions made the SAS's task of intelligence gathering much easier and more accurate.

The Gulf War proved that GPS receivers could withstand adverse weather conditions, were easy to use and were reliable, aided night movement, and worked well with laser designators. Accurate to within 25m, the next generation GPS receivers – the Precise Lightweight GPS Receiver (PLGR) – promises to be accurate to within 16m.

AIRCRAFT

The very name of the SAS – Special Air Service – reveals how important aircraft (both fixed-wing and helicopters) are to the Regiment. They are invaluable for the insertion, extraction and re-supply of long-range patrols.

O n the night of 16 November 1941, some 65 officers and men of L Detachment, SAS Brigade, boarded five twin-engined Bristol Bombay aircraft with their weapons, bombs and rations at Bagoush airfield in North Africa. Despite the fact that a gale was blowing the unit's commander, Captain David Stirling, decided the operation would go ahead. It was L Detachment's first mission and he and his men wanted to prove their worth to British military headquarters in Cairo. Their mission was to attack the airfields at Tmimi and Gazala and destroy Axis aircraft.

The heavily laden Bombays lifted off and headed out to sea in an effort to avoid enemy flak. Their fuselages were filled with men and equipment and the temperature was freezing because the doors had been removed. Two hours later the slow-moving aircraft headed inland, to be greeted by a hail of anti-aircraft fire. Worse, however, was that the sandstorm had obliterated the landmarks the pilots were relying on to make an accurate drop. This meant the men were dropped off target and the wind scattered the 'sticks'. As they drifted to the ground the problems got worse. Some men landed badly and were injured, others, unable to release their 'chutes immediately, were hurt when they were dragged across the desert floor by the wind after landing. Equipment containers were lost and the whole venture had to be abandoned.

The C-130 Hercules long-range transport aircraft is the workhorse of the RAF. It is also widely used by the SAS, mainly for parachute drops. Note the aerial refuelling probe.

FIXED-WING AIRCRAFT

SPECIAL FORCES AIRCRAFT

Despite its first disastrous association with aircraft and parachutes in November 1941, the SAS, true to David Stirling's belief that his men should be able to reach their targets by land, sea or air, persevered with training its recruits in parachuting. This practise has continued down to the present, and parachute training is now an integral art of the Regiment's Continuation Training. Each SAS 'Sabre' Squadron, for example, has one Air Troop specialising in all aspects of parachuting.

Aircraft are now an integral part of many special forces operations. Sometimes it is just not possible to insert units into operational areas by any other means. Therefore, aerial delivery is the only alternative. Apart from parachuting in men, the SAS also uses aircraft for supply, and for evacuating units or wounded individuals. What are the qualities aircraft need for special forces work?. First, their range should be good as they will often be called upon to fly out-of-the-way routes to their destinations to cut down the chances of being detected by enemy radar and aircraft, as well as anti-aircraft defences. Fortunately, the addition of aerial refuelling probes to modern aircraft means their range can be extended substantially. Second, short take-off and landing (STOL) qualities and the ability to use rough airstrips are essential for some of the aircraft supporting SAS-type operations, particularly if they are operating in jungle areas. Third, good fuselage capacity for both troops and equipment (something that converted World War II bombers, for example, did not have) is very important, as is ease of loading and unloading such materiel. Fourth, they must be reliable, rugged and be able to withstand operating in extremes of temperature, from the heat of the desert to the cold of the arctic.

In aircraft such as the C-130 Hercules transport aircraft and the CH-47 Chinook helicopter, the SAS has access to aircraft that possess these attributes and can perform a wide variety of missions. In addition, their airframes and avionics are being continually modified and up-graded to improve their performance, giving the Regiment an all-weather, long-range aerial insertion and re-supply capability.

Britain entered World War II with no aircraft suitable for parachute operations, and so, even for the drops into France in the days and weeks after D-Day, SAS men were still being dropped from converted bombers, such as the Whitley, Albermarle and the Halifax. Only the latter was a success in the role.

After the war the aircraft used by the SAS in Malaya and Borneo were largely undistinguished in their performance and suitability for airborne operations. The Valetta, Hastings and Beverley all had their faults. The first two, for example, only had side doors which made loading them a nightmare. It was only with the coming of the C-130 Hercules that the SAS, as well as the Parachute Regiment, had an aircraft that was truly suited to support airborne operations.

Albermarle This aircraft was used by the SAS in World War II, specifically to drop teams into occupied France in the days following D-Day. Originally designed as a twin-engined bomber-reconnaissance aircraft, it was later converted to pull gliders and drop paratroopers. In the months leading up to D-Day, the SAS Brigade was stationed east of Kilmarnock, Scotland, and all its men received training or refresher courses in parachuting.

Men jumping from an Albermarle did so through an exit area – called the 'bath tub' – situated in the belly of the aircraft. The soldiers sat on a ledge above the hole and, when the signal to go came up, would slip off and push themselves through the gap, which was unfortunately shaped like a coffin, taking care not to smash their faces on the sides as they did

Above right: The Bristol Bombay. Five of these aircraft were used on the SAS's first operation in November 1941. The mission was a debacle, not least because the Bombays were blown off course. Below right: The Valetta. Its rather awkward shape was reflected in its nickname: the 'flying pig'.

so (a man who misjudged his exit could have his nose broken and, if he was really unlucky, lose all his front teeth – this painful experience was jokingly known as 'ringing the bell'). Theoretically the Albermarle could take up to 10 paratroopers, though with each man fully equipped this dropped to four or five. Of largely wooden construction, the Albermarle was an unpopular aircraft with both aircrew and passengers alike. Despite this, some 600 were built in total.

Interestingly, there grew up a close relationship between Albermarle crews and the SAS in the weeks leading up to the D-Day landings, when the aircraft were being used in Britain to train SAS soldiers in parachute skills to prepare for theri insertion into France. Many RAF crews wanted to try parachuting themselves and so, despite it being against regulations, SAS teams dropping from aircraft were often joined by their Royal Air Force comrades.

Type: glider tug and special transport
Manufacturer: Armstrong Whitworth
Powerplant: two 1590-horsepower Bristol Hercules air-cooled piston engines
Range: 2100km
Maximum speed: 412km/hr
Armament: two 7.7mm Vickers 'K' machine guns in dorsal turret

Above: The Andover was used by the SAS in the late 1960s as a tactical transport aircraft. Its low-pressure undercarriage tyres meant it could take off and land from unprepared airstrips.

Andover Used extensively by the SAS as a tactical transport aircraft from the late 1960s, especially in the Middle East, Andovers are still in service today with the Royal Air Force, though reduced to the roles of calibration and general transport duties. The Andover has a strengthened floor and lengthened fuselage to accommodate wheeled vehicles. In addition, it has a rear loading ramp which, with its doors, can be opened in flight to facilitate the dropping of supplies to troops on the ground. The Andover also has a hydraulically adjustable landing gear which can be used to align the fuselage with vehicle tailboards, or enable vehicles to enter the aircraft via the ramp. Its Dart engines, large-diameter propellers and large-diameter, low-pressure mainwheel tyres means it can take off and land from airstrips only 457m long.

Type: military transport
Manufacturer: British Aerospace/Avro
Powerplant: two 3245-horsepower Rolls-Royce Dart turboprop engines
Range: 604km (fully loaded)

Maximum speed: 515km/hr
Armament: none

Auster Extremely capable light reconnaissance aircraft that was use throughout World War II and remained in service until the 1960s, taking part in the campaigns in Malaya, Aden and Borneo. During the Malayan Emergency (1948-60), SAS troops on the ground worked closely with the pilots of 656 Air Observation Post Squadron who flew Austers. The latter were used for anti-bandit reconnaissance which frequently meant lone flights over the jungle looking for camps and clearings (the latter often indicated areas used by the guerrillas for growing food). Following a sighting, the aircraft would report back to the infantry on the ground, which were often spearheaded by SAS patrols, who would attack the bases. It was a laborious, lonely task, but one which was vital in the war against the Communist Terrorists (CTs).

The SAS also used Austers for confirmation of patrol positions on the ground. For example, in October 1953 SAS troops were operating in the Cameron Highlands on the Perak-Kelantan border. They were there to build a jungle fort (fortified camps where the indigenous natives could live without being subverted by the CTs, and which acted as forward jungle bases for British forces). After reaching the approximate spot in the jungle, the patrol radioed for aerial confirmation of its location. An Auster then flew over and reported they were in the right place. Thereafter they began to construct the strongpoint which was later designated Fort Brooke.

The Auster was a high-wing monoplane which had its wing and steel tube fuselage and tail frame covered with fabric. The cabin accommodated two people – the pilot and the observer – who sat side by side. The last two versions of the Auster were designated Air Observation Post (AOP) 6 and AOP 9. The former, despite its more powerful engine and larger propeller, was in many ways a poorer performer than its predecessors.
Designation: AOP 9
Type: light liaison/observation aircraft
Manufacturer: Taylorcraft Aviation Company
Powerplant: one Blackburn Cirrus Bombadier 203 piston engine

Range: 389km
Maximum speed: 204km/hr
Armament: none

Beaver This utility transport aircraft had its maiden flight in 1947. It was used by the British in Malaya, Borneo, Aden and, later, Northern Ireland, and was extensively used by the SAS for re-supply duties until the 1970s. Of an all-metal construction, the Beaver was a high-wing monoplane with fixed landing gear. Its undercarriage could also be fitted with floats and skis, making it ideal for re-supplying troops operating in arctic conditions or in jungle areas, as the Beaver could land and take off from stretches of water. In addition, the aircraft had good STOL capabilities, allowing it to support clandestine operations.
Designation: DHC-2
Type: eight-seat utility transport
Manufacturer: de Haviland Canada
Powerplant: one Pratt & Whitney Wasp Junior R-985 radial engine
Range: 1180km
Maximum speed: 262km/hr
Armament: none

Beverley This four-engined transport entered service in the mid-1950s and was extensively used by the SAS in the Far East and Middle

Below: In service for nearly 30 years, the Beaver was used by the Regiment as a re-supply aircraft. It could take off from rough airstrips.

East. It was originally designed in 1944 for the expected airborne invasions of Germany and Japan in 1945-46, though the war ended sooner than anticipated and the aircraft was temporarily shelved. However, the Korean War (1950-53) showed that airborne troops were still needed and so the Beverley was put into production.

Capable of transporting 94 troops, 70 parachutists or 20,000kg of cargo, the Beverley had neither the range or payload capabilities to make it a truly long-range transport. Nevertheless, they served well enough between 1955 and 1967 and are remembered with some fondness by the aircrews who flew in them. Parachutists leaving the aircraft could do so in four simultaneous 'sticks' by using the port and starboard doors and by exiting from the left and right of the large boom door. However, the Beverley was mainly used by the SAS in the support role, dropping supplies to patrols operating in the jungles of the Far East or landing and off-loading equipment and/or picking up troops from rough, short landing strips in the Middle East (after landing it was customary for the aircrew to turn off three of the four engines while the cargo was unloaded or troops were taken on board). In Malaya, for example, SAS four-man patrols operating deep in the jungle were dependent on re-supply from RAF Beverleys as they only carried enough rations for 14 days. At two-week intervals, therefore, the aircraft would undertake air drops – the supplies leaving via the rear door – to the soldiers on the ground at a pre-determined drop site.

Type: four-engined transport aircraft
Manufacturer: Blackburn and General Aircraft Ltd
Powerplant: four Bristol Centaurus 2850-horsepower air-cooled turboprop engines
Range: 2090km
Maximum speed: 383km/hr
Armament: none

Bristol Bombay The aircraft used by the SAS in its first, disastrous, raid in North Africa in November 1941. It was in reality an obsolescent bomber that had been converted to the parachute role and the SAS had little success with it. When David Stirling had established the Special Air Service, the only aircraft he could lay his hands on for training purposes was a Bombay

loaned from 216 Squadron. For parachuting it was fitted with rails bolted to the floor, to which the parachutists attached their static lines by means of a dog-lead clip. When they jumped, the static line ran out from the parachute packs and, when fully extended, would break away the strings at the back of the pack. This would result in the parachute being forced out, snapping the remaining string and leaving the static line dangling from the aircraft. However, on the first parachute training session of the new unit the static lines of two men jumping side by side broke. As a result their 'chutes failed to open and they were both killed. The fault was immediately rectified and Stirling, aware of what the incident could do to morale, ordered that parachute training would re-commence the next day – and he jumped first.

This unfortunate accident was a foretaste of the ill-luck to come: in mid-November five of

Below: An RAF Beverley about to take off during the campaign in Aden. The aircraft supported SAS operations in the Middle East and Far East.

the aircraft were used to transport 65 SAS officers and men for a parachute drop against the enemy airfields at Tmimi and Gazala. However, owing to bad weather the men were widely scattered and the mission was a failure. Only 22 soldiers returned from this one operation, and it was the last time the SAS undertook a parachute operation in North Africa.

The Bristol Bombay was a twin-engined bomber/transport with a fixed undercarriage that first entered service in 1939. It usually had a crew of three and was capable of carrying 24 troops, though only around 15 paratroopers.

Type: bomber/transport aircraft
Manufacturer: Short & Harland Ltd
Powerplant: two Bristol Pegasus 1010-horsepower air-cooled engines
Range: 1415km
Maximum speed: 309km/hr
Armament: two Vickers 'K' machine guns, one in the nose turret and one in the tail turret

Dakota The Douglas C-47 was the most famous transport aircraft of World War II. The first models were laid down in 1932 and the first flight took place three years later. Simple, robust and able to take off from rough airstrips, the Dakota was capable of carrying 28 troops, 20 paratroopers or a payload of 3538kg. The aircraft was widely used by the SAS after the D-Day landings, when parties of men and loads of equipment were dropped behind enemy lines. It was still being used by the Regiment 10 years later in Malaya, when the highly dangerous tactic of 'tree jumping' was devised. This entailed men parachuting onto the jungle canopy, from where they would use ropes to lower themselves down to the jungle floor (which could be 30m further down). In addition, Dakotas were used to support more conventional operations. In July 1954, for example, 177 SAS soldiers were parachuted into the the thick jungle east of Ipoh to attack Communist Terrorists (CTs) in their bases. Clearings had been prepared for the SAS troops by RAF Lincoln bombers which had flattened large tracts of the jungle with bombs. On the ground the SAS were supported by four infantry battalions.

The four-month operation only resulted in the deaths of 15 CTs, though many enemy supply dumps and camps were also located.

The Dakota was a low-wing monoplane which had a stressed-skin construction and fabric-covered control surfaces. The lower half of the two main wheels remained exposed after they had been retracted into the engine nacelles. The aircraft usually had a crew of three: pilot, co-pilot and radio operator.

Type: transport aircraft
Manufacturer: Douglas Aircraft Company
Powerplant: two Pratt & Whitney R-1830 1200-horsepower air-cooled engines
Range: 1112km
Maximum speed: 370km/hr
Armament: none

Above: The Dakota was used by the SAS to drop teams into France after D-Day in World War II and, later, into the Malayan jungle.

Halifax A four-engined bomber with a crew of seven that was used by the SAS after 6 June 1944 to drop men and supplies – the aircraft was capable of dropping jeeps and trailers from its bomb-bay – into occupied northwest Europe. The jeep was packed into a wooden cradle which had air bags underneath to cushion the impact when it hit the ground (each jeep required four parachutes). For such drops the aircraft's bomb-bay doors were removed and a long beam fastened inside. The crated jeep, rigged with a complicated arrangement of crash pans and struts, was then attached to the beam to spread the load. Obviously this external load had an adverse effect on the aircraft's performance, reducing it considerably and making it sluggish to fly. Generally, however, the process worked and the SAS were supplied with many jeeps in this fashion, though not everything always went smoothly. During Operation 'Houndsworth' (conducted by A Squadron, 1 SAS, in eastern France between June and September 1944), one jeep dropped from a Halifax broke free from its cradle and crashed to the ground, resulting in a large crater (the hole was so deep that the men on the ground had an easy task burying the wreckage).

As an interesting aside, many SAS operations in France and the Low Countries after June 1944 were supported from RAF Station 1090 based at Down Ampney, Gloucestershire. However, the method of getting SAS teams in the field supplied was tortuous. It was unfortunate that the SAS Brigade possessed no aircraft of its own because all aerial transport arrangements had to be coordinated by I Airborne Corps and 38 Group RAF at Netheravon and Special Forces Headquarters. This meant the SAS had to 'bid' for aircraft – there were never enough to satisfy all needs – which frequently resulted in aircraft being allotted elsewhere at the last moment. This invariably meant both SAS and RAF personnel rushing round trying to finalise routes, supplies and men, and liaise with the units across the Channel.

Most Halifaxes for such operations were under the command of 38 Group and flew from airfields in Wiltshire and Oxfordshire. The Marks AIX and AIII were used by airborne forces, the former being specially modified to carry 16 paratroopers (who exited the aircraft through a large hole in the floor).

Type: heavy bomber
Manufacturer: Handley Page
Powerplant: four Rolls-Royce Merlin 1390-horsepower liquid-cooled engines
Range: 1577km
Maximum speed: 426km/hr
Armament: two .303-inch Browning machine guns in the nose turret; four in the tail turret; and two in manual beam positions

Above: Hercules aircraft based at RAF Lyneham are used to support SAS operations.

Hastings This aircraft superseded the Valetta and saw service in the 1950s, being used by the SAS in Malaya and Oman. Though paratroop jumps were undertaken from Hastings aircraft, it was mainly used by the Regiment in the re-supply role. One particular example illustrates the complexities of dropping equipment to men on the ground. In November 1958, D Squadron, 22 SAS, was on the Jebel Akhdar, northern Oman, and advancing against royalist rebels. Reaching the edge of the plateau, the SAS established a foothold despite being shot at by rebel snipers. Requesting aerial re-supply, a Hastings appeared overhead and dropped several containers. However, they were dropped from an altitude of 600m instead of 150m. As a result, when the 'chutes deployed many of them drifted off the edge of the plateau and were lost. In addition, others 'Roman candled' and plum-meted to the ground, smashing their contents to pieces. Worse was to follow a few days later when some mortar ammunition was dropped. Despite the Hastings dropping its load from 250m, some of the containers had been badly packed. As a result, some of the boxes broke free and crashed to the ground. The high explosive (HE) rounds had, unfortunately, been packed alongside white phosphorus shells and, as the latter started to burn fiercely, the HE shells got hot and started to explode. Needless to say, the drop was a total disaster.

The Hastings, which had a crew of five, had a two-wheel undercarriage. Its main drawback were its side-loading doors and lack of rear doors which made loading stores and pallets a complete nightmare.

Type: transport aircraft
Manufacturer: Handley Page
Powerplant: four Bristol Hercules 1675-horsepower air-cooled engines
Range: 6840km
Maximum speed: 560km/hr
Armament: none

Hercules The long-range transport aircraft currently used by the SAS, and one of the most durable transport designs since the C-47 Dakota. The Regiment's air transport needs are catered for by an RAF special forces squadron based at RAF Lyneham, Wiltshire, which includes Hercules aircraft in its inventory. The Royal Air Force today operates some 60 C-130 Hercules transports. They are based on the American C-130H model but have a number of differences: they contain British components and equipment, such as freight floor lashing points and avionics suites; they have inflight refuelling probes (called Hercules C.Mk 1P); they are equipped to act as refuellers; and some have stretched fuselages which improve their payload capabilities (desig-nated Hercules C.Mk 3).

The SAS used Hercules transports during the Falklands War of 1982, when both men and pallets were, on at least one occasion, dropped into the freezing Atlantic Ocean and then picked up by Royal Navy ships. Soldier 'I', an SAS sergeant, was one of them: 'I was in the ready position: right hand gripping the parachute static line, left hand resting on the top of my reserve...I moved closer still to the edge. The deafening roar of the aircraft slipstream made all conversation impossible. My head was raised and turned to the right, watching, waiting for the red warning light to turn to green. My rear leg was braced, ready to launch me over the edge of the tail-gate.'

Travelling in the fuselage of a Hercules can be extremely uncomfortable, as the engine noise is deafening and only webbing seating is usually available. Nevertheless, the C-130 is a very capable aircraft, its winning edge provided by the thought that went into its design. Turboprop propulsion, for example, resulted in more power for less weight. Pressurization of the cabin and fuselage enabled flight performance to be exploited at all altitudes. High-strength alloys were used in its construction; the cargo hold was given a level floor to facilitate unloading onto

**Above: Stirling bombers were widely used to drop
SAS teams into France in the days and weeks after
D-Day. The parachutists dropped through a large
hole in the floor of the fuselage.**
**Left: A Lysander with Italian partisans in 1945. Its
STOL qualities made it ideal for clandestine work.**

Type: long-range heavy transport
Manufacturer: Lockheed
Powerplant: four Allison T56-A-15 4508-horsepower
turboprops
Range: 9072kg
Maximum speed: 618km/hr
Armament: none

trucks; the tricycle landing gear was specifically
designed so the aircraft could use rough airstrips
(the aircraft's large paddle-blade propellers
means it can also lift heavy loads off these strips);
radar and full-span thermal de-icing give it an
all-weather operation capacity; and the rear
ramp door can be opened in flight for heavy
dropping. There is no doubt that the Hercules,
which is usually served by a crew of four, will be
used by the SAS for many years to come.

Lysander An aircraft most closely associated
with the Special Operations Executive (SOE) in
World War II, the bulky single-engined
Lysander was also occasionally used by SAS units
in 1944-45 which were operating behind enemy
lines. It was sometimes used to evacuate
wounded personnel, downed Allied airmen, or
Resistance leaders to England. In total,
Lysanders delivered 293 agents and their

passengers into France, and brought out more than 500 individuals.

The Lysander was a truly STOL aircraft, having a high-lift wing, full-span splats, large trailing-edge flaps and ailerons. The crew usually consisted of just a pilot, as the navigator's seat was often occupied by the passenger.

Type: two-seat tactical reconnaissance aircraft
Manufacturer: Westland
Powerplant: one Bristol Mercury XII 890-horsepower piston engine
Range: 966km
Maximum speed: 369km/hr
Armament: two .303-inch machine guns in wheel fairings; two .303-inch machine guns in the cockpit

Skyvan During the SAS campaign in Oman (1970-76), moving from one location to another was frequently undertaken by either aircraft or helicopters. This was for two main reasons: it was quicker, and the few roads that did exist were often mined by the guerrillas of the People's Front for the Liberation of the Occupied Arabian Gulf. Thus, SAS troopers and *firqat* personnel (irregulars trained by the SAS) were often transported in Omani Air Force Skyvan aircraft. As Colonel Tony Jeapes, commander of the Regiment in 1974, states: 'I flew into Barbezum [Oman] by Skyvan, that excellent flying truck developed by Short & Harland of Belfast. Sturdy, simple and easy to fly, the Skyvan became the work horse of the Dhofar war.'

The Skyvan has a high-aspect ratio wing mounted high on the fuselage and a full width rear door which can be opened during flight for a paratroop drop. The aircraft has a crew of two and can accommodate up to 19 passengers. Its ability to land on rough airstrips proved very useful to the SAS in Oman, and the aircraft is still in Omani service.

Type: STOL light transport aircraft
Manufacturer: Short Brothers & Harland
Powerplant: two Garrett TPE331 715-horsepower turboprops

Left: The Vickers Valetta, an aircraft used by the SAS in Malaya, Oman and Borneo for both parachute drops and aerial re-supply.

part of Operation 'Kipling', describes the risks involved when parachuting from a Stirling: 'As we struggled to fasten our leg-bags, the RAF despatcher and flight engineer flung open the folding doors above the jumping hole. I moved to the edge of the hole and looked down at the moonlit French countryside moving slowly past...'Chute open. Release leg-bag. It had jammed. As I tugged at it, the rope came free and, snaking wildly, wrapped itself around my hand. I felt a finger break.'

This four-engined bomber had a crew of seven and was a very long aircraft. However, because it was sluggish and had a poor ceiling, it was unpopular with aircrews, being especially vulnerable while carrying out daylight bombing.

Type: heavy bomber
Manufacturer: Short Brothers
Powerplant: four Bristol Hercules 1595-horsepower engines
Range: 4828km (Mk V)
Maximum speed: 435km/hr
Armament: two Browning .303-inch machine guns in the nose turret; four in the tail turret; early versions also had two in a remote control ventral turret

Range: 386km
Maximum speed: 325km/hr
Armament: none

Stirling At end of 1943, the Stirling, because of its slow speed and poor manoeuvrability, was obsolete as a heavy bomber and so was transferred to the airborne forces. Used to replace the ageing Albermarles, they were fitted with glider tow hooks and it was as glider tugs that they were mainly used. However, some were converted to accommodate paratroopers, being fitted with a large hole in the floor. Capable of carrying 22 paratroopers, Stirlings – the Mk V version – also dropped a number of jeeps to SAS parties on the ground in France in the autumn of 1944. The advance party for Operation 'Houndsworth', consisting of men from A Squadron, 1 SAS, was dropped from a Stirling in June 1944, the aircraft taking off from Fairford, Gloucestershire. Captain Derrick Harrison of 1 SAS, dropping into France in August 1944 as

Valetta First produced in 1947, the Vickers Valetta saw service until the mid-1960s and was used by the SAS for parachute and supply drops in Malaya, Oman and Borneo. It was a bulbous mid-winged, twin-engined aircraft which had almost the same load capacity as a Dakota. However, it had a major drawback in that the main spar of the wing ran across the forward end of the load compartment in a box 457mm high and 305mm wide. Everything had to go over the box which meant it was impossible to drop loads by roller conveyor. Called the 'flying pig', the Valetta had a crew of four and was able to carry 20 paratroopers.

Type: transport aircraft
Manufacturer; Vickers
Powerplant: two Bristol Hercules turboprops
Range: 2250km
Maximum speed: 276km/hr
Armament: none

Section 2
HELICOPTERS

Helicopters have, in many ways, revolutionised the battlefield and this is as true for the SAS as it is for other ground forces. The helicopter has a number of unique qualities compared to most other aircraft that make it a useful military tool: it can take off and land vertically, hover, fly at low speeds, and make severe turns and lateral manoeuvres. This means helicopters can operate independently of runways and can land and take off from any reasonably level surface. However, there is a price to pay for these qualities: helicopters are mechanically complex; they are inefficient in terms of load-carrying capability for the fuel used because they rely totally on power lift; they have relatively low speed because of the limitations of rotor aerodynamics; and they are aerodynamically unstable.

Nevertheless, the helicopter is ideally suited to many specialised military tasks: transport, liaison, scouting, reconnaissance, casualty evacuation, as well as a host of more specialised duties such as anti-submarine warfare and electronic warfare. The SAS first employed helicopters in Malaya during the Emergency (1948-60), where they undertook such roles as evacuating civilian and military wounded, landing patrols and delivering presents for local aborigines, and supplies to patrols on the ground. Helicopter pilots in Malaya performed some remarkable feats and there quickly grew up an excellent relationship between the pilots (particularly those of 55 Company, Royal Army Service Corps) and the SAS.

An example of the type of work performed by the helicopter crews is the operation conducted by 37 men of D Squadron, 22 SAS, commanded by Major Harry Thompson, in the Telok Anson swamp, southwest of Ipoh, Malaya, in February 1958. The objective was to kill or capture a group of Communist Terrorists (CTs) led by Ah Hoi. The men parachuted into the area but one of them, Trooper Mulcahy, injured his back badly on landing and had to be immediately evacuated. The helicopter came in and, at great risk, hovered near the ground, its rotors touching the trees. However, such was the

skill of the pilot that the man was successfully evacuated. Other pilots were not so lucky. Sometimes tail rotors would catch on trees and logs and the aircraft would be forced to crash-land. There were also fatalities. In May 1963, for example, during the Borneo campaign, a helicopter carrying, among others, Major Ronald Norman, the second-in-command of the Regiment, and Harry Thompson, at that time Operations Officer, crashed; tragically, all on board were killed.

However, helicopters also came into their own during this war. The task facing the SAS in Borneo was a daunting one, as it had to provide cover for the whole of the 1500km-long border. A 'step-up' drill was devised whereby, once an Indonesian incursion had been detected, an SAS patrol would radio for infantry reinforcements to be flown in by helicopter and landed on a cleared landing zone (in jungle areas these were usually created by using explosives and machetes). The patrol would then guide the infantry to an ambush site to await the enemy.

During the SAS presence in Aden (1964-67), the helicopter was again invaluable for transporting patrols to and from the combat zone. The Regiment established itself at Thumier, near the Habilayn airstrip, and on the edge of the Radfan. From Habilayn, Wessex helicopters would take off carrying SAS soldiers on reconnaissance and ambush missions.

Nearly 20 years later the Regiment was still using Wessex helicopters, only this time it was in the freezing conditions of the South Atlantic. The Falklands War was to witness the SAS making use of a variety of helicopter types, as teams were inserted from British ships onto East and West Falkland and, prior to that, landed on South Georgia. To date, little is known concerning SAS operations during the 1991 Gulf War against Iraq. However, it appears that the

Above right: A Belvedere in the Radfan, mid-1960s. Its performance in the desert was poor.
Below right: A Sea King drops SBS soldiers onto the British Embassy in Kuwait, February 1991.

112

Regiment employed Chinook and Sea King helicopters to insert men into Kuwait and Iraq, as well as relying on parachute drops.

A109 Two of these Italian-built helicopters were captured from the Argentinians during the Falklands War and were subsequently refurbished in the UK by the firm Mann Aviation (a further number of A109s were later purchased from the manufacturer in Italy). They are now reportedly in service with the SAS. The model in question, the A109A, has good performance and relatively cheap running costs and can carry out a variety of roles including counter-insurgency, anti-armour, transport and reconnaissance.

Type: utility and special transport helicopter
Manufacturer: Agusta
Powerplant: two Allison 250-C20B 420-horsepower turbines
Range: 565km
Maximum speed: 311km/hr
Armament: none (although can be fitted with TOW anti-tank weapons)
Payload: 898kg

Belvedere This was the first British tandem-rotor helicopter (under this configuration the two rotors are fore and aft and rotate in opposite directions to reduce torque) and was used by the Regiment in Aden (1964-67) and Borneo (1963-66). It had originally been designed as a naval helicopter, but the RAF had a requirement for a personnel and paratroop transport and a casualty evacuation helicopter which could also lift heavy loads on an external sling. The engine and gearbox were arranged to allow the aircraft to make a safe landing in the event of either engine or synchronizing shaft failure. However, the Belvedere required a great deal of maintenance and did not perform particularly well in the desert conditions of Aden.

Type: short-range tactical transport helicopter
Manufacturer: Bristol/Westland
Powerplant: two Napier Gazelle NGa 1465-horsepower turboshafts
Range: 740km
Maximum speed: 222km/hr
Armament: none
Payload: 2722kg

Chinook The CH-47 Chinook (British models are designated HC 1) is an extremely rugged medium-lift transport helicopter currently in service with the SAS. It has a twin-tandem rotor configuration and a ramp built into the rear of the fuselage to facilitate the loading of vehicles and pallets of equipment. In addition, the fuselage is totally watertight, allowing amphibious landings (a dam built in the cargo bay means the Chinook can also land on water with the ramp open). On land the aircraft's large, low-pressure tyres means it can operate from soft surfaces.

More than 15 per cent of the Chinook's airframe is manufactured from composite materials to reduce weight, while its rotor blades are made from glassfibre and Nomex and can withstand a hit from a 23mm cannon round. Other features include night-flying capabilities, electronic and infrared countermeasures. The Chinook has a crew of three and can carry up to 44 passengers or 24 stretcher cases and four attendants for casualty evacuation.

The Chinook was widely used by American and British forces during the 1991 Gulf War against Iraq, and it seems highly likely that SAS soldiers used them to move around the theatre of operations. As the aircraft can carry large loads slung beneath its fuselage from three load-carrying points, it is safe to assume that the Regiment's Light Strike Vehicles were also transported by Chinooks, either British or American.

Type: medium-lift transport helicopter
Manufacturer: Boeing Vertol
Powerplant: two Avco-Lycoming T55-L-712 turboshafts
Range: 2058km
Maximum speed: 287km/hr
Armament: none
Payload: 13,437kg

Dragonfly Built under licence by Westland from the US firm Sikorsky, RAF and Royal Navy Dragonfly helicopters supported SAS units on the ground during the Malayan Emergency.

Right: A number of Agusta A109s, similar to this one, are now in service with the SAS. They can carry up to seven passengers.

They were particularly useful for delivering supplies and, using basket stretchers, casualty evacuation. The main drawback to the Dragon-fly was the lack of room in its narrow fuselage. This meant that if two crew members were carried (with one operating the winch), anyone being rescued or evacuated had to be carried on external litters, making them vulnerable to enemy small-arms fire.

Type: general purpose helicopter
Manufacturer: Westland (under licence from Vought-Sikorsky)
Powerplant: one Pratt & Whitney R-985 450-horsepower engine
Range: 579km
Maximum speed: 171km/hr
Armament: none
Payload: 474kg

Gazelle During the early evening of 14 June 1982, a Royal Marines Gazelle helicopter flew into Port Stanley, East Falkland, to negotiate the surrender of the Argentinian forces throughout the Falkland Islands. On board the aircraft were two SAS soldiers, Lieutenant-Colonel Mike Rose, the commander of the Regiment, and Captain Rod Bell, a Spanish-speaking Royal Marine who acted as Bell's interpreter. Following cease-fire negotiations, the Argentinians signed the surrender document to bring the war to an end.

The Gazelle was widely used in the Falklands campaign, the aircraft being armed with 68mm rocket pods and cabin-mounted GPMGs. Though primarily a frontline observation and reconnaissance helicopter, it was also used in the Falklands for casualty evacuation and currently in Northern Ireland is used to move military and civilian personnel rapidly from place to place (Gazelles were used to evacuate SAS soldiers after the ambush at Loughall in May 1987). It has a crew of two and is capable of carrying up to four passengers.

Type: light observation, reconnaissance and liaison helicopter
Manufacturer: Aerospatiale/Westland

Right: This Chinook helicopter, flown by the RAF's 7 Squadron, was used to support special forces operations during the 1991 Gulf War.

Above: A Royal Navy Dragonfly. In Malaya they were useful for supplying SAS units on the ground and for casualty evacuation. The civilian version of the aircraft was called the Widgeon.

Powerplant: one Turbomeca Astazou IIIN2 643-horsepower engine
Range: 670km
Maximum speed: 264km/hr
Armament: none standard, but has provision for pod mountings (see above)
Payload: 918kg

Lynx Designated AH-7, this anti-tank and liaison helicopter is used by SAS teams to move quickly around Northern Ireland. Though not technically an aircraft designed for special forces, the Lynx is fast and highly manoeuvrable and can carry up to nine passengers. As such, it is ideal for SAS operations in Ulster.
Type: anti-tank, liaison and command helicopter
Manufacturer: Aerospatiale/Westland
Powerplant: two Rolls-Royce Gem 43-2-2 1120-horsepower engines
Range: 420km
Maximum speed: 177km/hr
Armament: eight TOW anti-tank missiles
Payload: 1766kg

Puma Introduced into British service as a replacement for the Westland Whirlwind and the Bristol Belvedere, the Anglo-French SA 330 Puma medium-lift helicopter has proved itself to be one of the finest models in its class. RAF Pumas have polyvalent air inlet filters – a forward-facing inlet for each engine. These are capable of deflecting objects such as ice breaking free from the nose, while other, smaller, holes around the side filter sand-sized particles.

The Puma has a crew of three and its large cabin can accommodate up to 16 fully equipped troops or 20 men without equipment. In addition, loads of up to 3200kg can be carried underneath the aircraft's fuselage over short distances. These qualities make it ideally suited to transporting and inserting SAS teams and/or casualty evacuation (there is room for six stretchers and seats for six other wounded).
Type: transport helicopter
Manufacturer: Aerospatiale/Westland
Powerplant: two Turbomeca Makila IA1 1877-horsepower turboshafts
Range: 1630km
Maximum speed: 278km/hr
Armament: none
Payload: 4800kg

Sea King The Westland S61 was widely used by the SAS during the 1982 Falklands War and the 1991 Gulf War. In the former many SAS teams were inserted onto both East and West Falkland by the Sea Kings of No 846 Squadron, Fleet Air Arm, based on the carrier *Hermes*. D Squadron, for example, conducted two heliborne raids, the first against the Argentinian airfield on Pebble Island and the second against enemy forces in the Darwin/Goose Green area as a diversion to cover the main landings taking place at San Carlos Water. A typical flight is described by Soldier 'I': 'The overloaded Sea King helicopters of 846 Squadron took off at precisely 1800 hours. They flew low and fast, skimming across the darkness of San Carlos Water, heading for Falkland Sound...We swept across the undulating terrain of East Falkland and then enemy-occupied West Falkland.'

The Sea Kings of 846 Squadron are optimized as assault transports and are designated Sea King HC.Mk 4. Other roles for

Above: A British Gazelle in the Gulf. In Northern Ireland they are used as fast transport for civilian and military – including SAS – personnel.

British Sea Kings include airborne early warning and anti-submarine warfare, as well as search and rescue. As the aircraft have to operate in all weathers, they are fitted with a complete avionics suite including doppler navigation radar, auto-pilot and an auto-hover system. The voluminous fuselage can hold up to 19 fully equipped personnel or six stretchers for casualty evacuation.

Type: assault helicopter
Manufacturer: Westland (under licence from Sikorsky)
Powerplant: two Rolls-Royce Gnome 1660-horsepower turboshafts
Range: 1230km
Maximum speed: 208km/hr
Armament: can be fitted with rockets and rocket pods
Payload: 3324kg

Scout The first turbine-powered helicopter of the British Army Air Corps, the Scout entered service in 1963. As soon as it did so it was used by the SAS to transport patrols (having the capacity to carry up to five passengers in addition to two crew). As such it saw service in Borneo, Aden and in the Falklands, and is still in Army Air Corps service. Capable of mounting 7.62mm machine guns and anti-tank guns, it can also be fitted with external stretcher cases for casualty evacuation. As it is extremely stable in the hover mode, the Scout is an ideal platform for troops who have to abseil to the floor if the aircraft cannot land.

Type: light utility/anti-tank helicopter
Manufacturer: Westland
Powerplant: one Rolls-Royce/Bristol Nimbus 105 701-horsepower turboshaft engine
Range: 488km
Maximum speed: 211km/hr
Armament: 7.62mm machine gun and 68mm aerial rocket pods
Payload: 929kg

Sycamore The Bristol Sycamore helicopter was mainly used by the SAS for casualty evacuation in Malaya, Oman and Borneo. The aircraft had a light alloy cabin section and a stressed-skin tail-boom attached to a central engine and gearbox mounting. The main drawback was the Sycamore's low passenger-carrying capacity. It could only transport five people, two of whom were the crew. Nevertheless, it did provide the Regiment with a helicopter capable of evacuating wounded men from the battle zone.

Type: search and rescue/light transport helicopter
Manufacturer: Bristol Aeroplane Company
Powerplant: one Alvis Leonides 550-horsepower radial engine
Range: 510km
Maximum speed: 204km/hr
Armament: usually none, though some were fitted with a Bren gun in the cabin doorway
Payload: 812kg

Left: Predominantly an anti-armour helicopter, the Lynx's manoeuvrability, high speed and passenger-carrying capability make it ideal for troop lifts and evacuation operations. It is used by the SAS for such missions in Northern Ireland.

Wessex Originally built under licence from Sikorsky – which used the designation S-58 – the SAS has used Wessex helicopters since the early 1960s, mainly for the transportation of troops, casualty evacuation and the movement of supplies. During the Borneo campaign the SAS used 'stripped out' Mk Is, but by the time the Regiment was engaged in the retaking of South Georgia in 1982, the models in use were Mk 3s and 5s. The former had automatic tracking equipment for accurate position-keeping out of sight of ships or the shoreline, while the latter was a transport version.

On 21 April 1982, three Wessex helicopters dropped Mountain Troop of D Squadron, 22 SAS, onto Fortuna Glacier, South Georgia. The unit's task was to establish a number of observation posts around Leith and Grytviken. However, because of the weather conditions the men did not travel far before being forced to camp for the night on the glacier. The next day the commander of the party was forced to request immediate evacuation, fearing for the lives of his men, exposed as they where to the unremitting cold. The radar-equipped Wessex 3 from HMS *Antrim*, flown by Lieutenant-Commander Ian Stanley, led two Wessex 5s from the tanker *Tidespring* in blizzard conditions and in high turbulence. On the first attempt the aircraft were forced to return, having failed to reach the men. The second attempt was more successful, the party being found and loaded onto the aircraft. However, moments after taking off both Wessex 5s crashed because the weather had closed in. One of those in a Wessex, Corporal Davey of D Squadron describes what happened: 'The Mark 3 put in a shallow right-hand turn, height probably about 200-300 feet, the first Mark 5 started the turn but was hit by a sudden whiteout in which the pilot lost all his horizons and we crashed into the ice.' Returning to *Antrim* with a heavily loaded aircraft, Stanley then returned to the glacier twice and picked up all the men on the ground on the second attempt. For his flying that day Stanley won the Distinguished Service Order.

The SAS still employs Wessex helicopters in Northern Ireland for troop-carrying duties (they can carry up to 16 fully equipped men). Despite its age, the Wessex is still one of the most

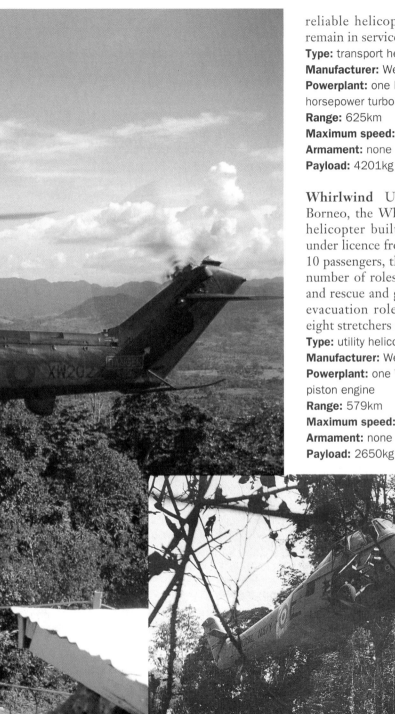

reliable helicopters around, and one that will remain in service until the end of the century.

Type: transport helicopter
Manufacturer: Westland (under licence from Sikorsky)
Powerplant: one Rolls-Royce Coupled Gnome 1550-horsepower turboshaft
Range: 625km
Maximum speed: 212km/hr
Armament: none
Payload: 4201kg

Whirlwind Used by the SAS in Malaya and Borneo, the Whirlwind was a reliable transport helicopter built by the British firm Westland under licence from Sikorsky. Capable of carrying 10 passengers, the S-55 Whirlwind was used in a number of roles: anti-submarine warfare, search and rescue and general transport. In the casualty evacuation role the aircraft could carry up to eight stretchers and one attendant.

Type: utility helicopter
Manufacturer: Westland (under licence from Sikorsky)
Powerplant: one Wright R-1300 800-horsepower piston engine
Range: 579km
Maximum speed: 180km/hr
Armament: none
Payload: 2650kg

Above: A Wessex helicopter during the campaign in Borneo. They are still used by the SAS to transport troops in Ulster.
Left: The Puma tactical transport helicopter.

Section 3
PARACHUTES

Since World War II the SAS has employed parachuting as a means of inserting units into enemy territory. During 1941-45, the Regiment used the Irvin X-Type model, a simple device for reaching the ground in one piece. It remained in use until the 1960s, when it was replaced by the Irvin PX1 Mk 4, which is the current British Army static-line parachute (static-line parachuting is where the soldiers exit the aircraft and the 'chute is deployed at a predetermined height by a line connected to the aircraft). Models currently in use include this 'chute, the PX Mk 5 and the PR7 reserve.

LEARNING SPECIALIST DRILLS

Units such as the SAS, although its members are initially taught static-line parachuting at RAF Brize Norton, Oxfordshire, do not usually employ this method in its operations. Rather, SAS teams use either High Altitude, Low Opening (HALO) or High Altitude, High Opening (HAHO) parachuting techniques.

Pioneered by RAF parachute instructors, these systems of parachuting are designed to allow teams of specialists to drop onto a target area undetected by enemy radar and personnel. The training is, like that for the static-line course, conducted at RAF Brize Norton. However, before it starts each man must pass an RAF medical, as well as the static-line course. The course concentrates on a large amount of ground work in which students learn to freefall and deal with problems – a soldier's equipment during a jump can weigh anything up to 60kg and this can send him into an uncontrollable spin if he exits the aircraft badly or collides with a colleague during the descent.

During the course the students are split into teams, and each team member must complete 50 freefall jumps from a variety of aircraft and helicopters in both day and night conditions in different parts of the UK. Their equipment is highly classified and constantly changing, though it is known that the small oxygen bottles used by individual troopers during the descent provide up to 10 minutes of air.

HALO PARACHUTING

During a HALO descent a soldier usually leaves the aircraft at an altitude of 10,000m and freefalls until he reaches an altitude of 760m, when his 'chute deploys automatically. The equipment used is classified but is probably the 'mattress' and steerable type of parachute such as the GQ 360 nine-cell flat ramair canopy model (the more cells allow greater weight to be carried and give greater flexibility in windy conditions). The great advantage with HALO descents is that the team can land together, which means valuable time on the ground is not wasted rounding up the unit (it must be remembered that most HALO drops are conducted at night).

A soldier's personal load during a HALO descent would include oxygen breathing kit, main 'chute and reserve, helmet with headset, altimeter, bergen rucksack and personal weapon.

HAHO TECHNIQUES

HAHO parachuting is another freefall technique designed for use by special forces. The equipment used is almost identical to that employed for HALO jumps. However, a trooper making a HAHO jump exits the aircraft and deploys his 'chute at an altitude of around 8500m. He then makes a gentle, and silent, descent to the ground. Using this method he can float over long distances (thereby lessening the chances of being spotted by enemy forces), all the time controlling the rate of descent and direction. In addition, the 'chutes can be stalled on reaching the ground to enable the soldier to make a safer landing.

Both HALO and HAHO were reportedly used by the SAS during the 1991 Gulf War against Iraq, though as yet the reports are unconfirmed. What is certain is that SAS soldiers are highly skilled in the use of these two parachuting techniques.

Above right: A HALO parachutist. The breathing apparatus is essential when exiting the aircraft at altitudes in excess of 10,000m.
Below right: British Paras before a static-line jump.

VEHICLES

In World War II the SAS used jeeps to great effect in North Africa and in northwest Europe. Since then, highly mobile and heavily armed vehicles have played an integral part in many of the Regiment's operations, most notably in the 1991 Gulf War.

D avid Stirling, the founder of the SAS, had from the beginning always insisted that his unit should be able to arrive at its target by air, land or sea. This would ensure that it always had a degree of operational flexibility, thereby increasing its chances of success. He envisaged a unit that would combine minimum manpower demands with maximum possibilities for surprise, believing that 200 properly trained and equipped men, fighting as five-man teams, could attack 30 different targets simultaneously on the same night.

The first operation mounted by the SAS was in North Africa in November 1941. It was a parachute drop behind enemy lines that had as its objective the destruction of Axis aircraft on two airfields; it was also a complete disaster (see Chapter 5). Subsequent missions were more successful, relying as they did – up to the middle of 1942 – on the transport and goodwill provided by the Long Range Desert Group (LRDG). The standard procedure was for the LRDG to transport SAS soldiers and their bombs to the target and then evacuate them after the raid.

The next SAS Land Rover? Hereford has been evaluating a number of these Special Operations Vehicles (SOVs), giving rise to speculation that they will enter service with the Regiment.

TRUCKS

The SAS has been associated with trucks since its creation. At first it used those of the LRDG, and the latter was beneficial to the SAS in three ways. First, it provided the transport to and from the target (parachute drops had been temporarily abandoned in North Africa as being too unreliable). Second, the LRDG had carried out extensive reconnaissance and mapping of much of the vast desert area of North Africa, and so was familiar with the best routes to individual targets. Third, travelling with the LRDG gave David Stirling and his men first-hand experience of long-range desert warfare and the attributes men and vehicles needed to travel in the demanding conditions; knowledge that would later be put to good use when the SAS had its own desert transport.

Vehicles for units such as the SAS – like the men they transport – must be able to operate in any terrain and weather conditions, and this is as true today as it was in World War II. For manufacturers this can create a number of problems. Consider the task. They must build a vehicle that can operate in conditions that range from intense heat where sand and dust can have a corrosive effect, to temperatures so low that grease and petrol freezes solid. Repairs and maintenance can also be a problem, especially if the supply lines are long. However, it is very much a learning process. In the desert of North Africa during World War II, for example, the LRDG got round spares difficulties by cannibalising vehicles. The enemy may have things to offer too: in North Africa the British had initial problems with the containerisation of petrol, oil and lubricants (POL). However, these were overcome when quantities of the standard German liquid container were captured. These were copied and nicknamed 'Jerry Cans'.

Today each 'Sabre' Squadron has a Mobility Troop that specialises in light vehicle warfare. SAS soldiers might be transported to the theatre of operations in ships or parachute from aircraft, but once on the ground they invariably move around in vehicles unless, of course, they are in a jungle environment. Although the 1991 Gulf War is still shrouded in secrecy as far as SAS operations are concerned, it is known that patrols used Land Rovers and Light Strike Vehicles to move around the deserts of Iraq and Kuwait, and the weapons and equipment these vehicles carried differed little to those fitted to World War II SAS jeeps.

Less glamorous than machine gun-equipped jeeps and dune buggies, though no less essential, are the various trucks the Regiment has used since its creation. They are used to transport supplies, equipment and men, though on the modern battlefield the truck has been made redundant to a certain extent by the helicopter. Nevertheless, the SAS continues to employ standard British Army trucks for the day-to-day duties that are an integral part of any military formation's operational procedures.

WORLD WAR II

In the summer of 1941, the grandly named L Detachment, Special Air Service Brigade (numbering six officers and 60 men), was training at Kabrit, North Africa, to prepare for active service. In charge of whipping the men into shape was Lieutenant 'Jock' Lewes. To prepare them for parachute drops, Lewes had the men rolling backwards from the rear of a moving 15-cwt truck. Not surprisingly, the result was a crop of broken bones and this particular training method was soon halted. Nevertheless, the SAS would be closely associated with truck transport during the first few months of its existence, specifically those employed by the Long Range Desert Group (LRDG). Many of the ideas and methods pioneered by the LRDG were later taken up by the SAS and, indeed, by the Allied armies as a whole.

The principal LRDG vehicle was the 30-cwt Chevrolet two-wheel drive truck. Usually armed with a Lewis gun and sometimes a Browning M1919 machine gun (later the Lewis was

Above right: SAS soldiers and Bedouin in Oman, late 1950s. Note the light truck in the background.
Below right: A modern Bedford four-ton truck.

Renault one-ton truck

replaced by a Vickers 'K'), the vehicles were also fitted with sun compasses, wireless sets, sand channels and water condensers.

The sand channel was, like most good inventions, a simple device but one which was vital for vehicles moving through the desert. Called the 'steel channel', it was first used by Major Ralph Bagnold (the founder of the LRDG) during a trip across the Sinai in 1926. It consisted of a corrugated iron trough which had originally been designed for roofing. However, it was also ideal for getting vehicles out of soft sand and mud.

The procedure could be tortuous. Johnny Cooper, one of the 'Originals' of L Detachment who took part in many SAS jeep operations, describes it thus: 'When a truck got bogged down, the drill was as follows. The crew would pick themselves up and unload as much of the gear on board as possible. Then we had to pull out the sand mats and sand trays and start to dig out the wheels. The mats went under the front wheels and the steel channels under the rear ones. With the engine churning in low gear, all hands pushed until the rear wheels were standing firmly on the channels. Then we would get the channels from the other vehicles and start feeding them in as our truck inched its way forward.'

The water condenser kept vehicle water consumption to a minimum and was an essential piece of equipment for long-range desert travel.

The overflow pipe from the radiator was blocked off and a rubber tube was directed from the radiator into a water can that was bolted to the running-board and half-filled with water. When the water in the radiator boiled the steam condensed in the can, and when the water in the radiator had stopped boiling the vacuum would suck more water out of the can. Thus, if the joints in the system were air-tight, it was possible for the vehicle to travel long distances without fresh water. Both sand channels and water condensers were fitted to SAS vehicles in North Africa.

WORLD WAR II TRUCKS

By mid-1942, the SAS had its own jeeps and so was not dependent on the LRDG for transport. However, trucks continued to be used for hauling supplies to base camps and those situated behind enemy lines, such as at Jalo, and to accompany groups raiding enemy airfields. One of those used, the Bedford QL, had four-wheel drive for rough terrain, but could also disengage the front drive for use on hard roads to ease the overall wear on tyres and gearbox. Another truck used by the SAS during the North African campaign was the Ford F60, a vehicle that utilized the Canadian Military Pattern Chassis.

Ford F60
Powerplant: one Ford V-8 95-horsepower petrol engine
Maximum speed: 80km/hr

Bedford MK four-ton truck

Range: 270km
Payload: three tons

Bedford QL
Powerplant: one Bedford six-cylinder 72-horsepower petrol engine
Maximum speed: 61km/hr
Range: 370km
Payload: three tons

POST-WAR TRUCKS

While retaining most of the features of their World War II predecessors, most modern military trucks have several notable differences: they are capable of carrying greater loads (usually four to five tons instead of two or three); they have larger tyres and wheels for greater ground clearance; they have all-wheel drive to aid cross-country mobility; and petrol engines have been replaced by diesel ones, the latter being more fuel efficient and less likely to catch fire.

The most important medium truck in British service since 1945 has been the Bedford model, at first the three-tonner and then the four-tonner. The British Army selected the Bedford RL 4x4 vehicle in the 1950s as one of its standard 3000kg trucks (being uprated in 1968 to 4000kg). By 1969, when production ceased, over 70,000 models had been produced for the civil and military markets. A competition was held in the 1960s to find a successor to the RL.

The winner was the Bedford MK which was based on the civil 4x2 TK truck chassis. For military use it was given a different engine, all-wheel drive and larger tyres. The MK is still in service today. It has an all-steel, fully enclosed forward control cab, though many vehicles have a roof opening on which a 7.62mm machine gun can be mounted. It can be fitted with a wide variety of extras including single or rear dual wheels, troop seats each side of the cargo area, a five-speed gearbox (the standard model is four-speed), and power-assisted steering.

The Bedford has seen wide service with the SAS in the Middle East and the Far East, and continues in use with the Regiment (other trucks in use include the Renault one-ton truck). On a more mundane level, Bedfords are used to transport potential recruits to and from their endurance marches over the hills and mountains situated near the Regiment's base at Hereford. For many SAS soldiers, and those that failed to make the grade, the memory of a waiting Bedford four-tonner at the end of a gruelling day will be a poignant one.

Bedford MK
Powerplant: one Bedford six-cylinder 130-horsepower diesel engine
Maximum speed: 77km/hr
Range: 560km
Payload: 4530kg

Section 2
LIGHT VEHICLES

Units such as the SAS require light vehicles that are reliable, can take a lot of punishment, and can move at great speed if required. As with most things, a compromise must be reached when special forces select light vehicles. For example, high speed can only be achieved at the expense of payload, which includes armament, and on extended operations it might not be possible or desirable to reduce payload. Consider the SAS in North Africa during World War II. Both it and the LRDG were operating in an area approximately the size of India. This meant that the distances to be covered could be immense. Based at oases behind enemy lines, for example at Jalo, raiding parties would venture forth and strike the enemy where he least expected it. Highly mobile vehicles meant that hit-and-run raids were the order of the day. Using Chevrolet trucks and US-made jeeps, the SAS and LRDG covered thousands of kilometres, their vehicles equipped with sand tyres, special filters, larger fans and radiators, condensers, sand shovels, jerry cans, machine guns and compasses and sextants for desert navigation.

As well as high mobility, both units realised their vehicles also had to have the capacity to carry enough food, ammunition, water and fuel to support long-range missions (SAS jeep patrols were often accompanied by trucks carrying extra supplies). Therefore light vehicles used by special forces tend to be a compromise between payload capacity and size and speed.

LAND ROVERS

There are two vehicles that are traditionally associated with the SAS. One is the World War II American-made jeep, the other is the Land Rover. It is indeed fortunate that the Regiment has had, and continues to have, use of the latter as Land Rover vehicles are the best soft-skinned machines in the world. The fact that the SAS, which can select any vehicles for its use, has always chosen Land Rover models is testimony in itself to the qualities of these machines.

The first military Land Rovers, the Series I, were built between 1948 and 1958. At first only petrol engined versions were available but, later, diesel models were introduced, and from 1954 a long-wheelbase Series I was also brought out. The Series II was introduced in 1958, with both petrol and diesel versions available. In 1968 a lightweight Series II appeared which was designed for use with airborne units, being designated the Lightweight, the Half-Tonne or the Airportable. It had cut-down wings and removable panels to allow it to be slung underneath the fuselage of a helicopter. The Series III was produced between 1971 and 1983, the only major difference being the repositioning of the headlamps to the front wings to meet British Ministry of Transport vehicle regulations. The bulk of these vehicles had petrol engines, though some, such as those used by the Royal Navy, were diesel powered. The Forward Control or One Tonne version was built between 1975 and 1978, its main role being an airportable artillery tractor. From 1984 the Ninety and One-Ten Series were produced and these vehicles are the current workhorses of the British armed forces. A stretched version, the One-Thirty, is currently in service as an ambulance and artillery tractor. Just before the August 1990 Iraqi invasion of Kuwait, Land Rover renamed its Ninety/One-Ten/One-Thirty vehicles the Defender.

The British Army has traditionally used short-wheelbase Land Rovers because they are more manoeuvrable than their long-wheelbase counterparts. However, units such as the SAS traditionally have employed long-wheelbase versions because of their greater carrying capacity. The most famous of these vehicles in service with the Regiment was the long-range desert patrol vehicle, nicknamed 'Pink Panther', used since the early 1960s. Basically a Series II 109-inch (length) chassis model, it had no doors, was equipped with smoke canisters and had a spare wheel mounted over the front bumper. It

Above right: SAS 'Pink Panthers'.
Below right: Land Rover One-Ten Desert Patrol Vehicles are optimized for special forces use.

was painted pink – hence the name – to blend in with the pink haze frequently seen in the desert. This vehicle was used by the SAS all over the world, and versions of the 109 were also spotted being driven by troopers in Northern Ireland in 1969, though not painted pink!

What makes Land Rovers the best light utility vehicles in the world? First, they are powerful and agile at low speed in mud and sand, and they are relatively fast for road travel. Second, they have excellent power-weight ratios and good underbelly clearance, while their even weight distribution means they are effective on soft surfaces. Third, their overall serviceability is excellent, and their aluminium bodywork can take a lot of punishment – when called for, routine field damage can be repaired with a panel hammer.

The SAS One-Ten Land Rover (110-inch chassis) uses a coil-spring suspension similar to that employed on the Range Rover which gives a comfortable ride (to incorporate this feature required the redesign of the whole chassis). In addition, disc brakes were added to the front wheels and the vehicle has a smaller turning circle than the 109-inch Series. There is no reason to doubt that the One-Ten will give the Regiment excellent service in any terrain (the SAS also used several Nineties in the Gulf which were fitted with weapon mounts, had additional storage space and were called 'Dinkies').

Armament for Land Rover vehicles can vary, though modern variants tend not to be bristling with a multitude of machine guns like World War II SAS jeeps. This is not to say that the modern Land Rover cannot be formidably armed if required. For example, it can be fitted with a front 7.62mm machine gun and a variety of weapons mounted on the rear. The latter include twin 7.62mm machine guns on power-assisted mounts and with a swivel seat, and a single 0.5-inch Browning heavy machine gun, or a 7.62mm chain gun. Almost any combination of weapons can be carried according to the mission requirement.

In early 1992, information became available which suggested that the SAS was 'interested' in the Land Rover Special Operations Vehicle (SOV). Combining the firepower of the Light Strike Vehicle with the payload of the Land Rover, it can carry six men and mounts machine guns front and rear, in addition to the twin mount on the pulpit. Based on an intercooled turbo-diesel Land Rover One-Ten, the SOV also carries a Light Anti-armour Weapon (LAW), an 81mm mortar, a 51mm mortar, two personal weapons, two submachine guns, two grenade launchers plus spare ammunition for all the above. In addition, Milan, TOW or a 25mm cannon can be mounted on the rock-steady pulpit weapons platform. The SOV certainly packs a powerful punch.

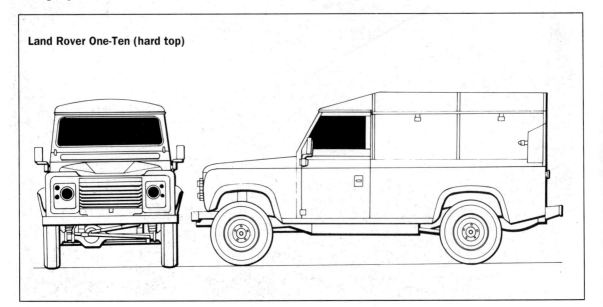

Land Rover One-Ten (hard top)

'Pink Panther'
Powerplant: 2286cc petrol engine
Maximum speed: 100km/hr
Range: 500km
Armament: usually two 7.62mm GPMGs

One-Ten
Powerplant: 3528cc petrol engine
Maximum speed: 120km/hr
Range: 750km
Armament: usually two 7.62mm GPMGs

SOV
Powerplant: 3500cc petrol engine
Maximum speed: 120km/hr
Range: 750km
Armament: mix of GPMGs, 51mm and 81mm
mortars, LAW 80 and 30mm cannon

Below: A World War II SAS jeep operating in northwest Europe in late 1944. Note the three Vickers 'K' machine guns and the armoured glass to protect the driver and front passenger.

JEEPS
During the late afternoon of 26 July 1942, 18 jeeps carrying 50 SAS soldiers left their desert base 100km from the North African coast and headed for the enemy airfield at Sidi Haneish, situated 66km from the sea. Driving in open formation, the journey lasted four and a half hours, with frequent stops to mend punctures. Approximately two kilometres from the airfield the party split into two columns. Each jeep was armed with twin Vickers 'K' machine guns mounted front and rear, and some had an additional Browning machine gun.

Racing onto the airfield, the jeeps drove past lines of parked enemy aircraft, strafing each one as they passed with machine-gun fire. The night sky was soon illuminated by rows of burning aircraft. Sporadic and inaccurate enemy fire failed to halt the attackers as the jeeps wheeled around the perimeter of the airfield, destroyed more aircraft and shot up several buildings. By the time the SAS had retreated there were 40 aircraft on fire or lying wrecked on the ground. The cost

to the attackers had been one man killed and two jeeps destroyed.

The World War II SAS jeep was a potent fighting machine. First delivered to North Africa in July 1942, the US-made design became one of the most famous military vehicles of the war. Those used by the SAS in North Africa were stripped of all unnecessary equipment to allow them to be loaded with water condensers, sand mats, ammunition, water and food. In addition, jeeps bristled with guns, usually four Vickers 'K'

guns often supplemented by a single Browning machine gun. The fuel tanks were also enlarged, an essential requirement over the distances that had to be covered in North Africa.

The American Willys jeep was fast, highly manoeuvrable and mobile, though a little uncomfortable for its three occupants (some SAS jeeps only had a crew of two, making them slightly less cramped). From mid-1942 until the end of the war the SAS employed the jeep with great success. The jeeps used in northwest

Towards the end of 1944, SAS troops operating in France began to receive a new and updated version of the jeep. These vehicles had armoured perspex screens that could stop a .303-inch bullet in front of the driver and front gunner. The whole of the front of the vehicle was covered in armoured plate, and some were equipped with a wire-cutting device above the front bumper. Armament varied, though most were fitted with twin Vickers at the front, plus a Bren gun for the driver, and twin Vickers mounted on the back. Occasionally a jeep would have a Browning 0.5-inch heavy machine gun at the front and/or a Lewis gun mounted on the rear. Each jeep was also equipped with grenades and ammunition for the crew's side arms. All in all, each vehicle was a highly mobile platform that could lay down a devastating amount of firepower.

One of the largest SAS jeep operations of World War II was Operation 'Archway', conducted between 25 March and 10 May 1945. Undertaken by between 300 and 450 men and 60 and 75 jeeps (sources vary regarding the numbers involved), the mission, involving elements from both 1 and 2 SAS, was commanded by Lieutenant-Colonel Brian Franks. The SAS objective was first to support the Allied airborne landings – Operation 'Varsity' – on the east bank of the Rhine, and then to carry out a deep penetrations into northeast Germany ahead of the main forces. The ultimate objective for 'Frankforce', as it was known, was Kiel.

Throughout the operation the SAS encountered sporadic resistance, occasionally encountering SS troops. The story of the drive to Kiel was recorded by Sergeant-Major Bob Bennett of D Squadron, 1 SAS, who took part in 'Archway'. His comments regarding the jeeps are particularly interesting: 'There was a petrol tank under the passenger seat and two others in the back, which made it a bit cramped for the rear-gunner. They made it difficult for him to bring his gun to bear on a target.' In the second week of the operation the SAS reached Hanover, by

Europe in 1944-45 differed to the ones used in North Africa. The condensers were dispensed with and they generally carried less supplies because operating ranges were far shorter – they operated either from bases behind the lines or were near the frontline. In addition, unlike in North Africa, the RAF dropped supplies to SAS parties on the ground; indeed, by 1944 jeeps themselves were being dropped by parachute from the bomb-bays of aircraft such as Halifax bombers.

this time driving well ahead of the troops of the 21st Army Group. Bennett continues: 'The jeeps always came first. Whenever we halted for the night, each crew checked the tyres, gave the engine the once over and sorted out any faults. Everyone was mechanically minded and many men had been with jeeps since the desert days.' The SAS reached Kiel on 3 May. The dash across Germany had cost 'Frankforce' a total of seven killed and 27 wounded.

Truck, Utility, 4x4 Jeep
Powerplant: one Willys 60-horsepower petrol engine
Maximum speed: 100km/hr
Range: 460km
Payload: 1000kg

'DUNE BUGGIES'
A new type of military vehicle, used operationally for the first time in the 1991 Gulf War, is the 'dune buggy' light attack vehicle. Used by

both the US Special Forces and the SAS, specific details concerning the exact deployment and operations of these vehicles is not yet known.

This type of vehicle first appeared in the early 1970s in response to military needs for a small, very light, deep-attack or reconnaissance vehicle. As such it was a move away from the heavier long-range vehicles such as the SAS Land Rover and the heavily laden jeeps of World War II. The advantages of the smaller model are

not hard to see: it can be carried either slung beneath the fuselage of a helicopter or even carried inside a CH-47 Chinook; in the field it is easier to conceal; it can use small tracks and access points; it can be manhandled by its crew if necessary; it has a low silhouette – aided by its open-frame construction – which means a reduced radar and thermal signature; and it is more mobile and so harder to hit. However, there are certain drawbacks to the 'dune buggy': most importantly, it cannot carry large loads of ammunition, fuel, supplies and water and it is, therefore, dependent upon a base, constant air supply or a larger 'mother truck'.

The fast attack vehicle can fulfil many roles: command and control, weapons carriage, reconnaissance, forward observation/laser designation for artillery and naval gunfire and anti-armour missions. Long-range strike and reconnaissance operations require each vehicle to have a minimum payload capacity of around 500-600kg, usually split between food, water, ammunition and other stores (ammunition alone for such missions may take up 300kg, made up of 2000 small calibre rounds and 500 grenade rounds for example).

The SAS uses the Light Strike Vehicle (LSV) produced by the British firm Longline. It has a wishbone suspension, a high quality seamless steel tube chassis frame and four-wheel drive. The LSV can mount a combination of weapons including a Gecal 0.5-inch gatling gun, a 0.5-inch Browning heavy machine gun, twin Brownings, a 40mm M19 grenade launcher, a 30mm cannon and a 7.62mm GPMG. In addition, it can also carry a Milan anti-tank weapon, Stinger anti-aircraft missiles and can transport either a 51mm or 81mm mortar for ground use.

Light Strike Vehicle
Powerplant: one Volkswagen 1900cc engine
Maximum speed: 128km/hr
Range: 400km
Payload: 500kg

Left: A British Army trail bike in the Gulf. Because of their high mobility and speed, motorcycles are often used by SAS Mobility Troops to traverse difficult terrain.

COUNTER-TERRORIST EQUIPMENT

The SAS is the world's most effective hostage-rescue unit. The hardware used by the Regiment for such work ranges from the highly sophisticated to the very simple.

On 5 May 1980, 'Pagoda' Troop of the SAS stormed the Iranian Embassy in London to free hostages being held by six armed terrorists of the Democratic Revolutionary Front for the Liberation of Arabistan. The building was stormed simultaneously at the front and rear by the black-clad counter-terrorist soldiers, who had thrown in stun grenades and launched CS gas into the building before entering. Five of the terrorists were subsequently killed and the sixth wounded in the operation which, by any standards, was a remarkable success. Though one of the hostages had been killed by the terrorists during the assault, the rest were safely evacuated from the building.

The SAS's success at the Iranian Embassy was testimony to the effectiveness of the Regiment's counter-terrorist training and equipment. That the Regiment should be involved with such work was not really surprising; after all, the SAS had been fighting communist guerrillas and terrorists since the 1950s in Malaya. However, those operations were conducted far from the United Kingdom and called upon the traditional skills of the soldier. The terrorism that struck the West in the 1970s was different, and so called for a different response.

The equipment of the modern CRW soldier: respirator, High Power handgun, stun grenade and black assault suit.

141

Section 1
CLOTHING AND ASSAULT AIDS

The murder of 11 Israeli athletes at the 1972 Munich Olympic Games by the Palestinian group 'Black September' led to the creation of the German anti-terrorist unit GSG 9. In Britain, the atrocity led to the SAS assuming the role of a dedicated hostage-rescue unit and the establishment, in 1973, of a Counter Revolutionary Warfare Wing at Stirling Lines, the Regiment's UK barracks, at Hereford (since the 1960s, several senior SAS officers had been advocating that the Regiment prepare for anti-terrorist work). The Wing has a permanent staff of around 20 and, on a rotation basis, trains all members of the Regiment's 'Sabre' Squadrons in every aspect of anti-terrorism. Rapid entry and hostage-rescue skills, for example, are honed in the 'Killing House', specially constructed rooms that simulate the scenarios the SAS may encounter during a real hostage-rescue operation.

Bursting into rooms – which can be filled with smoke and/or CS gas – containing hostages and armed terrorists demands not only special human skills, it also requires specialist equipment and weapons. The latter need to work first time, every time, and they need to be lightweight, compact and accurate. The clothing worn by the soldiers also needs to be dependable, rugged, efficient and lightweight. It soon became apparent that ordinary military clothing, being bulky and inflammable, was totally unsuitable for hostage-rescue work. Therefore the Operations Research Wing was set up at Hereford to test, evaluate and design every type of equipment used by the Regiment for its counter-terrorist work.

Today the specialist needs of hostage-rescue units has led to the creation of a whole international industry to service those needs. Because of the covert work the Regiment carries out in Northern Ireland, it is highly secretive concerning its counter-terrorist clothing and equipment. The hardware listed in this chapter is not necessarily currently used by the SAS. However, there is a high probability that the Regiment's soldiers use equipment very similar to that described below.

I have limited the chapter in the main to the clothing and hardware used for hostage-rescue work. There is, however, another side to the SAS's counter-terrorist duties and that is its operations in Northern Ireland. In the main this consists of a deadly cat-and-mouse game played with the highly trained and well-equipped terrorists of the Irish Republican Army (IRA) and, to a lesser extent, the Irish National Liberation Army (INLA). This work involves surveillance – days on end lying in cramped, uncomfortable 'hides' in rural areas observing arms dumps or suspects – or plain clothes missions on the streets of Belfast or Londonderry, or, occasionally, confronting armed terrorists in ambushes. The work is unglamorous and dangerous, but vital, and it is carried out to the very highest levels of professionalism and dedication. SAS soldiers in Ulster wear both civilian clothes and military uniforms but they do not, as a general rule, wear beige berets or any other items that may identify them as members of the Regiment. This is to increase the mystique of the SAS in the Province, and to prevent identification of individual members of the Regiment by the press and terrorist groups.

THE REQUIREMENT

During a hostage-rescue assault SAS team members require protection from heat, fire, smoke and blast, as well as from the bullets fired by the terrorists (though the team relies on speed and surprise during the assault, there is no guaranteeing every terrorist will be overpowered before at least one of them manages to discharge his or her weapon at least once, if only accidentally). Therefore each team member must be protected against these threats. All assault suits and underwear are therefore made from flame resistant materials. The G.D. Specialist Supplies suit currently used by the Regiment is

Above right: 'Pagoda' Troop soldiers at the rear of the Iranian Embassy on 5 May 1980.
Below right: CRW weapons and clothing.

Above: GPV 25 body armour. It has complete wrap-around soft armour while there are hard ceramic composite plates front and back.

made from Nomex which gives a high level of protection. In addition, it incorporates an integral respirator hood and flame barrier felt pads in both the knees and elbows (the SAS reinforce the elbow and knee joints with Kevlar inserts). This gives protection against sharp objects and allows the wearer to crawl across hot surfaces. The level of protection can be increased substantially by wearing assault underwear underneath the suit. Fireproof gloves are also worn during the assault; as well as protecting hands and wrists, they ensure a continuous grip on weapons and other pieces of equipment.

Body armour 'As I pulled on my assault kit, a pain in my temple throbbed continuously. I looked down at the heavy Bristol body armour lying on the bench-seat next to my holdall. Fuck the high-velocity plates!, I thought, I'm not in the mood for training with that on today – and I

threw the ceramic plates back in the holdall. With the now much lighter body armour secure in place, I drew on my skin-tight aviators' leather gloves, cocked the action of my Heckler & Koch MP5, introducing a live round into the chamber, applied the safety-catch, carried out the same operation on my Browning pistol and realized I had begun to sweat. It was going to be a long, tedious day.' (Soldier 'I')

During an operation the need to protect assault team members from bullets and flying fragments is paramount, though it must be remembered that protection can often be at the expense of manoeuvrability. Military body armour had almost disappeared by the outbreak of World War I. However, that conflict sparked a revival of armour, at first by the wearing of steel helmets to protect soldiers from splinters and concussion, and later the issuing of body armour – rigid, overlapping plates to cover the upper and lower torso – to sappers and assault troops. During the inter-war years body armour, except for helmets, disappeared again, to be revived during World War II in the shape of 'flak jackets' worn by bomber aircrews, which consisted of steel plates inserted into an upper body garment. However, they weighed a great deal and were unsuitable for infantry soldiers. The use of body armour became more wide-scale with the introduction of 'soft' armour made of fibreglass or ballistic nylon. This affected the momentum of a projectile by spreading its impact over many layers. Useful against grenade or artillery splinters, such garments performed less well against high-powered bullets. The breakthrough in body armour came with the introduction of Kevlar, a lightweight fibre of very high tensile strength.

Units such as the SAS wear ceramic inserts in addition to Kevlar layers during hostage-rescue operations. This is to defeat all types of high-velocity and armour-piercing rounds, as well as standard ammunition. Dowty Armour-shield of the UK produces a range of general purpose vests and restricted entry vests for hostage-rescue work. They all incorporate the so-called blunt trauma shield which prevents the wearer being seriously hurt by a round that strikes him. Though armour may defeat a bullet, the latter may still cause a deep depression in the armour and so transfer a large amount of shock energy – blunt trauma – to the wearer. This can, in the worst case, result in the wearer's death. However, the blunt trauma shield, worn underneath the soft armour, absorbs and dissipates the shock energy over a wide area (a soldier hit by a round fired at close range will, despite the shield, still be knocked over and winded for a short while).

Armourshield's GPV (General Purpose Vest) 25, currently used by the Regiment, has soft armour which gives wrap-around protection and has extra high underarm cover to allow the wearer to return fire without exposure. The vest is 18mm thick including the blunt trauma shield. Over the vest hard armour – consisting of ceramic composite plates – can be worn, giving the user full protection against high-velocity, armour-piercing and all NATO and Soviet rounds. However, there is a price to pay in terms of weight. Dowty's larger ceramic plates, for example, weigh up to nearly 4kg each. Protec Armour Systems of the UK produces so-called uparmour plates that consist of a ceramic tile backed with a laminate and covered with a rubberised foam. They are slightly lighter, weighing up to 3kg. They, too, are designed to defeat high-velocity rounds.

Another company whose products are suitable for special forces operations, particularly for undercover work, is Meggitt Composites of the UK. The firm produces a wide range of goods including body armour, helicopter armour and bomb disposal suits. Its Type 18 armour jacket, for example, was designed with special forces in mind and is of a lightweight modular construction that gives the wearer excellent mobility. In addition, double curvature ceramic plates are available to give greater protection to the user.

Headgear At the storming of the Iranian Embassy in May 1980, the SAS headgear consisted solely of anti-flash hoods. None of the soldiers were wearing helmets. The lack of any head protection was a glaring omission that has since been rectified. Flash hoods offer some protection against heat, dust and smoke, but are useless against a bullet, fragments and falling debris. Hostage-rescue units were forced,

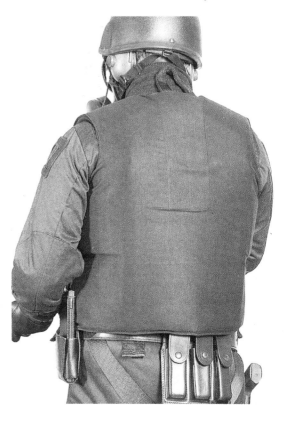

Above: Despite a weight penalty, ceramic plates are also worn on the back. This is to ensure the wearer has all-round protection.

therefore, to adopt some form of bullet-stopping and general head protection.

At first standard-issue military helmets were looked at. They were readily available and they had been tried and tested. However, they were soon discovered to be unsuitable for a number of reasons: they were too heavy, offered insufficient protection, and could be difficult to keep on the head during an assault. Therefore manufacturers set about designing helmets that fulfilled the needs of hostage-rescue units. What they came up with were helmets made from plastic, not steel, which could also be used if the wearer was equipped with a gas mask. Two west European units which employ such ballistic helmets are GSG 9 and the Italian counter-terrorist unit *Nucleo Operativo Centrale di Sicurezza* (NOCS).

Helmets, especially when fitted with a visor or worn in conjunction with a respirator, prevent dust, tear gas, smoke, debris and grit getting into

145

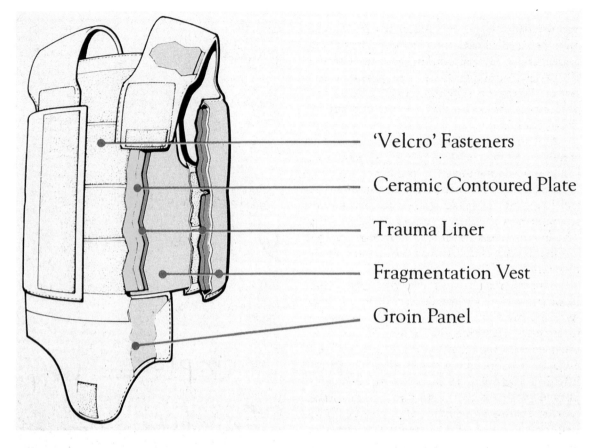

'Velcro' Fasteners

Ceramic Contoured Plate

Trauma Liner

Fragmentation Vest

Groin Panel

Above: A cut-away diagram of Armourshield's GPV 25 body armour. Note the built-in trauma shield that absorbs a bullet's energy.

the eyes – particularly if the wearer is entering a room after a stun grenade has been thrown in. However, they do have their drawbacks: some hostage-rescue teams feel they impede the time in which a soldier can acquire a target, and they can get in the way during a silent pre-assault approach.

The helmet currently used by the SAS is the AC100/1 model produced by the UK firm Courtauld's Aerospace Advanced Materials Division. Designed to be worn over a headset and respirator, it is made from multiple layers of ballistic-resistant composite materials. This construction gives it greater protection against small-arms ammunition than conventional military steel helmets. All the helmet's webbing and support systems are constructed from natural fabrics and high quality leather for comfort. In addition, it has an integral high

impact trauma system liner built in to dissipate the energy of any blow.

Respirators During a hostage-rescue operation the SAS team will often have to blow in doors and windows with explosives or shotguns, or smash them in with sledgehammers; they will most probably use stun grenades to disorientate the terrorists; and sometimes they will use CS gas and coloured smoke. Though the electricity and gas supply to the building they are entering will have been cut, there will still be combustible materials that may catch fire (at the Iranian Embassy in 1980, one of the SAS soldiers abseiling down the back of the building was burnt by flames when he became entangled in his rope). Such materials will produce smoke, often toxic smoke if the inside of an aircraft cabin catches fire (if all this seems far fetched it is as well to remember the assault made upon a hijacked Egyptian airliner by Force 777, an Egyptian counter-terrorist unit, in Malta in September 1978: a small charge designed to act as a diversion during the assault resulted in the cabin being filled with toxic smoke, killing many passengers). This will quickly combine with the CS gas and/or smoke fired in just prior to the assault. To move through this and still be able to perform their tasks, SAS soldiers must be wearing respirators.

At the Iranian Embassy in 1980, every member of 'Pagoda' Troop wore a respirator. Just as well. By the time the operation was over – 17 minutes – parts of the building were on fire and it was full of smoke. When terrorists' eyes are blinded by smoke they cannot breathe easily. The hostage-rescue unit has obvious advantages – provided the assault troops can breathe easily themselves.

The respirator currently in use with the Regiment is the SF10 produced by the UK firm Avon Polymer Products Ltd. It entered service in 1986-87, replacing the earlier S6 model. It provides full protection for the wearer and also ensures low breathing resistance – both for inhalation and exhalation – reducing overall physiological burden on the user, an important factor during the stress of a rescue. The respirator noseguide (nosecup) guides the inhaled air up the sides of the face and over the eyepieces to minimise 'fogging'. The filter gives protection against gases, aerosols and smoke, and the small oral/nasal chamber through which exhaled air is taken out of the respirator leaves only low levels of carbon dioxide (the canister can be mounted on either the left or right side of the facepiece according to user requirement).

The eyepieces are made of polycarbonate and are scratch resistant, resistant to chemical or solvent attack, and can also withstand impact damage and fragmentation. In addition, tinted lenses can be fitted to the outside of the respirator for protection against flash – an important consideration if stun grenades are used.

Two types of communications are possible with the SF10: direct speech at short range, and by radio, via a microphone mounted in front of the lips which can be linked by means of a communications harness to a radio transmitter. The total weight of the respirator is only 800gm.

Another type of breathing apparatus produced by Avon is the Special Operations Set,

Above: Abseiling skills are often crucial to the success of a hostage-rescue operation. Modern rigs allow soldiers to descend one-handed.

an air breathing system to allow entry into burning buildings or toxic areas. Similar in looks to a fireman's respirator, it consists of a specially adapted gas mask facepiece which can be worn beneath a helmet and can work as a normal air breathing system. Alternatively, in very toxic or low oxygen situations, the soldier can breathe from a pressurised air supply for 15 to 20 minutes depending on the size of cylinder carried on his back.

SUPPORT EQUIPMENT
In addition to the body armour worn by assault team members, each soldier will also be carrying extra equipment on his body such as spare magazines. There are a number of load-carrying assault vests currently available that can accommodate spare magazines, radios, stun or

Above: The AC100/1 composite helmet provides excellent head protection.

gas grenades, first aid kits and a knife (normally for cutting away any entanglements rather than for stabbing anyone!). Pictures of the SAS attack on the Iranian Embassy reveal that individual troopers usually carry their magazines on the hip, a typical arrangement being three Heckler & Koch MP5 magazines worn on the left hip, a Browning High Power handgun in holster on the right, and spare High Power magazines worn on the left thigh and right wrist, the latter for rapid magazine changes. Contrary to popular imagination, special forces units do not always tape a spare magazine to the one already in the weapon – the spare magazine can get covered in dirt (which causes severe feed problems when it is loaded, i.e. it jams the weapon), while two magazines interfere with the balance of the weapon and affect aiming and handling. In any case, tests have shown that a skilled soldier can change a magazine for one in a pouch faster than if two are taped together.

The Price Western Leather Company of the UK make a number of heavy duty Cordura webbing belts suitable for special forces operations, and it also markets a number of suitable holsters. Another firm noted for its holsters is the American company Bianchi International. It has a number of models designed for the military market, notably the tactical shoulder holster that allows a handgun to be carried under a jacket. Such an accessory would be useful for plain clothes work in Northern Ireland.

Abseiling equipment Police and military assault teams often have to descend quickly to effect an entry into a building. At Princes Gate, for example, the SAS abseiled down the rear of the building and entered via the back. Abseiling equipment is, therefore, an essential part of a hostage-rescue unit's equipment. There are three main components required for abseiling: a well-designed rope, harness and a descendeur (a metal device, clipped to the harness, through which the rope is threaded, thereby enabling the soldier to control his rate of descent). Rope used for hostage-rescue work has to be high quality material. At the Iranian Embassy, for example, one of the first men to abseil down the rear of the building became entangled in his rope and inadvertently broke a window with his foot. In addition, his dangling meant explosive charges could not be used to blow open the windows. This did not interfere with the ultimate success of the operation, but it could have had dire consequences. What had happened was that the SAS team had initially brought insufficient rope with from Hereford, and so new rope was purchased in London. This new nylon rope was of inferior quality and, during the assault, overheated because of the friction caused by the

weight imposed on it – it then quickly ravelled into a knot.

Descendeurs are an essential part of abseiling equipment. Models currently available include the Rollglis locking-brake system which can be controlled with one hand, allowing the other to hold a weapon. The Inter Risk Abseil 3 Speed Descendeur is a sophisticated device which can be hand-held for normal descents and brakes automatically when released. It can also be set for slow, medium or rapid descents. IKAR's AS1 allows the soldier to make a rapid

Below: Respirator hoods, shown here in SAS use at Princes Gate, are designed to give protection against blast and heat, and are made from Nomex.

Above: The SF10 respirator provides protection against gas and smoke and weighs only 800g.

descent at the rate of 5.5 metres a second if required, and the company also produces an abseil harness suitable for hostage-rescue operations.

Assault ladders As well as going down, counter-terrorist units may be called upon to ascend to effect an entry. The German GSG 9 team at Mogadishu in 1977, for example, used rubber coated assault ladders to to gain entry to the hijacked Boeing 737 aircraft, and units entering railway cabins and upper-storey windows will also need equipment to reach doors and windows. UK firm W.J. Clow produce a wide range of sectional assault ladders to facilitate entry into trains, aircraft and first- and ground-floor buildings. The ladders are

constructed of lightweight aluminium and are deeply serrated to give better grip to hand, foot and wall (their weight also means there will be no audible thud when they are placed in position). Clow's double width ladder can hold six fully armed and equipped soldiers at the same time and, most useful for rapid deployment purposes, all of its ladders can be fitted to the sides of roof of Land Rovers, Range Rovers and specially modified armoured personnel carriers.

Assault ladders usually have hooks at the top for extra grip; they can also be used for bridging purposes or as a sniper platform. Units such as the Special Air Service and other European counter-terrorist units have specifications relating to the height of wings and doors of various types of aircraft and trains currently in service, or other likely terrorist targets, so the right ladders are immediately available should the need arise.

Tools When one thinks of units such as the SAS, one's thoughts inevitably conjure up images of James Bond-type gadgetry. Whereas the SAS can call on some sophisticated equipment, particularly for surveillance duties, much of the hardware used can be surprisingly simple. After all, during a counter-terrorist operation the main requirement is for everything to work first time. At Princes Gate the SAS used sledgehammers to break the glass windows at the rear of the building to gain entry. Other tools carried by an assault team can include bolt cutters, wrecking bars, axes, glass cutters and grapple hooks.

Explosives and grenades To gain entry a team will often have to use explosive devices to blow in doors and windows. These so-called 'frame charges' are flexible and can be bent and shaped for ease of emplacement. The French firm SNPE make a rapid opening system which consists of a cutting detonating cord and a self-adhesive explosive strip charge. Accuracy Systems of the USA has devised explosive door cutters that can blow open hollow and solid core wood doors and standard industrial hollow metal doors. The cutters consist of charges wrapped in soft, flexible foam, enabling them to be bent and shaped according to requirements.

Stun grenades The stun grenade was originally designed by the SAS and has been successfully used by the Regiment and foreign hostage-rescue units. It is essentially a diversionary device that produces a blinding flash and loud bang – hence the name 'flash bang' – which disorientates the enemy and hopefully forces him/her to duck and keeps their heads down. They are available in single or multiple-bang versions.

Among many stun grenades currently on the market are those of the German firm PPT. Its Type A stun grenade is a flare and sound grenade which produces a vivid white flare that lasts for around 15 seconds. The Type B is a multi-report grenade that issues eight loud bangs in quick succession; and the Type C is a flare grenade only. Two British manufacturers of stun grenades are Royal Ordnance and the Scottish firm Brocks Pyrotechnics. The latter makes the

MX range of stun grenades comprising the MX5 which delivers five simultaneous flash/bangs; the MX8 which delivers eight bangs in a ripple action; and the MX7 which delivers a mixture of flashes, bangs and smoke.

CS gas CS in gas form can be an extremely useful tool to the hostage-rescue team, though its effectiveness has to be weighed against potential damage done to the hostages. Used by the SAS at the Iranian Embassy, the gas causes a severe burning sensation in the eyes with tears, coughing, and difficulty in breathing with a tightness in the chest. The eyes close involuntarily, the nose runs and moist skin burns. CS gas can be launched from anti-riot projectors or, contained in a grenade, can be thrown by hand. During a rescue assault team members will normally be wearing respirators, but the hostages will not and so it is important that they are evacuated as quickly as possible from the area if CS gas has been used.

Below: Assault ladders were used by GSG 9 at Mogadishu airport in October 1977.

WEAPONS AND AMMUNITION

The firearms carried by SAS soldiers during hostage-rescue operations are usually restricted to the Heckler & Koch MP5 submachine gun and the Browning High Power handgun, with the Remington 870 pump-action shotgun sometimes used to effect entries. However, for counter-terrorist operations in Northern Ireland the Regiment's troopers use a variety of weapons, chief among them being the SLR, silenced Sterling, Heckler & Koch 53, Ingram submachine gun, Colt Commando and the weapons used by the IRA – AK-47, Armalite and the M1 Carbine. On 23 February 1985, for example, three SAS soldiers ambushed three armed IRA terrorists – part of a five-man hit team intent on ambushing a police car – in Strabane, Northern Ireland. The SAS soldiers were all armed with 5.56mm Heckler & Koch 53 submachine guns. In the ensuing gun battle all three terrorists were killed in a hail of fire, though at least one of the SAS soldiers was forced to use his Browning High Power handgun when his submachine gun jammed. The firefight was very short, but the Heckler & Kochs, firing at a rate of 700 rounds per minute, put down a devastating barrage of fire. The subsequent autopsy revealed the three dead men – Charles Breslin, Michael Devine and David Devine – had been hit by 13 bullets, 28 bullets and five bullets respectively. One interesting point is the stoppage encountered by one of the SAS soldiers, proof that even the most finely engineered weapons can sometimes jam.

The criterion for the selection of weapons for hostage-rescue operations – and it is much the same for SAS operations in Northern Ireland – is the right equipment for the job in hand. This may sound obvious, but there are in fact few weapons that meet the exacting requirements for hostage-rescue work. Assault teams want guns that are reliable, accurate, compact, have full-automatic fire, and have good balance. It is useless, for example, to burst into a room full of hostages and terrorists armed with a British-built 7.62mm Self-Loading Rifle. Its length means it cannot be wielded effectively in confined spaces and it does not have a full-automatic fire capability.

The submachine gun on the other hand, especially the Heckler & Koch MP5, has the minimum weight and maximum firepower qualities that counter-terrorist units look for. For this reason it is the primary assault weapon for units such as the SAS. Each individual soldier must be highly skilled as exact shot placement is essential with a weapon capable of firing up to 900 rounds per minute. In addition, the weapon must be capable of mounting sights and lighting devices for low light conditions. There are currently only three submachine guns in production that are suited to hostage-rescue work: the MP5, the Uzi and the Beretta M12.

Handguns are usually the backup weapon during an assault, though often the point man will carry one as it allows him to hold, for example, a stun grenade in the other hand. In addition, handguns are ideal for use in confined spaces where it can be difficult to wield a submachine gun, such as in aircraft cabins. Handguns have an additional advantage for hostage-rescue work in that the user has to pull the trigger each time he wants to fire (apart from the Glock 18 model). This deters wild firing and encourages exact shot placement. Counter-terrorist units hardly ever use revolvers because they have a magazine capacity of only six rounds maximum, compared with 13 or more for a semi-automatic handgun.

AMMUNITION

As well as selecting the correct weapons and clothing, the counter-terrorist unit has to consider the type of ammunition to be used in a hostage-rescue situation. The widely-held view that as soon as a target is hit he or she instantly falls down dead is false. In fact, hitting the target is, in many ways, the least of the counter-terrorist soldier's problems. He has to ensure his

Above right: Royal Ordnance G60 stun grenades.
Below right: The Heckler & Koch MP5 submachine gun is used by the SAS for hostage-rescue work.

target is stopped before any harm can be done to himself and the hostages, and he will want to be assured that any bullets he fires at the target will not pass through the body and hit a hostage (snipers like to be in a position where they are shooting down at a target because, if the round goes through the terrorist's body, it will not travel far before hitting the ground). As standard-issue ammunition was quickly discovered to be inappropriate for use by assault teams in a hostage-rescue operation, specialist rounds had to be devised for such work.

It soon became clear that the design of ammunition for law enforcement and counter-terrorist operations was, and is, complicated by conflicting demands. In the first place there is a requirement for a bullet that will unfailingly drop the target in his or her tracks. This is not particularly difficult in itself, but the problem comes with the demand that the bullet should not pass through the target and hit somebody else and that it must not, in the event of a miss, ricochet off a hard surface and hit a hostage or innocent civilian.

Bullets and wounds There are basically two types of bullet used in a hostage-rescue operation: high-velocity sniper rounds and pistol ammunition, the latter being 9mm calibre in the case of the Special Air Service (ammunition used in submachine guns is essentially the same as that employed in handguns). Sniper bullets can travel at speeds in excess of 900 metres a second (high-velocity is classed as being any bullet with a velocity higher than 700 metres a second). When they hit the body they produce an effect known as hydrostatic shock: the pressure wave the bullet produces by displacement of water-carrying tissue. This results in a temporary cavity many times the size of the permanent cavity drilled by the bullet itself. The pressure wave damages tissue far from the wound track, and so organs can be destroyed that are not actually hit directly. In addition, secondary missiles – shattered bone fragments – create their own wound tracks using some of the transferred force of the bullet. Thus, despite small exit and entry wounds – the bullets tend to go through the body – high-velocity rounds can cause very severe internal injuries. If possible,

the sniper will try for a head shot because a high-velocity bullet that strikes any part of the brain cavity will kill the terrorist because it destroys the entire brain due to hydrostatic shock. Body shots to the torso come next if a head shot is not possible.

Other types of ammunition act differently when they strike the body. All bullets are spun in the barrel when fired to ensure accuracy. This is called 'rifling'. However, 5.56mm ammunition is not spun as much as 7.62mm ammunition. This means that the latter has greater long-range accuracy, but it also means that at short ranges a highly spun and more powerful 7.62mm bullet will go through a target and carry on going. The 5.56mm round, on the other hand, will often 'tumble' as soon as it hits the target because it is under-spun. The bullet fragments, particularly if it hits bone, and sends particles spreading in all directions causing severe wounds.

Handgun and submachine gun bullets generally travel at around 400 metres a second, far slower than rifle rounds (the Heckler & Koch MP5SD has a muzzle velocity of under 300 metres a second). The lower velocity means the bullets have less hitting power than rifle rounds. However, because they are used at close ranges – four to five metres during a rescue – they can still shoot through a body. In addition, the bullets are smooth and tapered to enable them to work in semi- or full-automatic weapons which also means they are more likely to pass through the body of the target. They also retain a large part of their energy as they pass through the body, and so can wound any hostage they hit.

Specialist rounds Faced with the problems concerning standard ammunition, manufacturers set about creating specialist bullets that had increased stopping power but would not pass through the body. They discovered there were five ways to achieve this. First, increase the size of the bullet. This was clearly impossible because the calibre of the weapon was fixed. Second, use a bullet with good wound channel capabilities, i.e. the wound channel does not close behind the

Right: Weapons such as this SIG-Sauer SSG 3000 sniper rifle fire high-velocity rounds that can inflict massive tissue damage on the target.

bullet but, rather, a core is created which causes the victim to lose blood quickly. However, these rounds tend to have a high jam probability. Third, employ hollow- or soft-point bullets which expand on impact and so increase the diameter of the round, causing it to stop in the body and dump all its energy (and, if it passes through the body, most of its energy will already have been transferred). The problem with 9mm ammunition is that its velocity is often too low to ensure bullet deformation when the rounds hit the body, and hollow-point high-velocity rounds can be broken up on objects before they hit the target. Fourth, use frangible rounds, i.e. bullets that break up when they hit the target. Finally, a more lethal round can be created by increasing a bullet's velocity and decreasing its weight. Thus the lighter bullet, despite having a high muzzle velocity, slows down quickly when it hits the target and stays in the body, transferring all its energy in the process. Most modern counter-terrorist rounds are either bullets that break up in the body, or ones that have some sort of hollow-point arrangement or unconventional shape. In addition, the use of composite

Above: The Heckler & Koch MP5K submachine gun weighs only 2kg empty and is only 325mm long.
Above right: Both shotguns and submachine guns can fire specialist anti-personnel rounds.
Below right: The High Power handgun can be loaded with a wide variety of ammunition types.

materials in bullet design has resulted in the development of more effective rounds.

'Dum Dums' Many specialist rounds are often talked about as being 'Dum Dum' bullets. However, this is quite incorrect. The 'Dum Dum' takes its name from the Dum Dum Arsenal on the outskirts of Calcutta, India, where it was invented by Captain Bertie Clay, Royal Artillery, the Superintendent of the Arsenal in the 1890s. It was a standard .303-inch lead-core bullet with the jacket removed at the tip to expose the lead core, thus allowing the bullet to 'mushroom' on impact, and it represents the British Army's first attempt to develop a specialist round.

The 'Dum Dum' bullet had been invented for a specific role: to improve the lethality of the

Above: Because of its reliability and accuracy, the Heckler & Koch MP5 submachine gun is used by SAS teams for hostage-rescue work.

.303-inch round against Dervishes and other fanatic natives who, often 'high' on hashish smoked before a battle, tended to ignore being drilled by a jacketed .303-inch rifle bullet! Known first as the Mark II Special and the Mark

III, it was used to great effect at the Battle of Omdurman (1898). However, it was soon discovered that there was a likelihood of the propellant charge blowing the lead core out of the rifle but leaving the nickel-steel bullet jacket stuck to the rifling, resulting in difficulties when trying to load the next round. Therefore the design was changed to a jacketed bullet with a hollow point, the hole being lined with a thin tube of jacket material; this expanded on impact and had much the same effect as the 'Dum Dum' but had no tendency to disintegrate in the bore. This became the Mark IV bullet and was soon followed by the Mark V, which did not have the tube lining to the hollow point.

However, the Hague Declaration of 1898 prohibited the use of expanding bullets in war and full jacketed ammunition has been the rule ever since. Actually the Convention relates only to wars between nations, and does not impinge on the armaments which can be used by police and internal security forces, a point conveniently forgotten by those who scream about police using illegal ammunition.

Modern specialist bullets Many manufacturers and specialist military and police units are very reluctant to discuss the types of ammunition they develop and use. The SAS, which pulls a veil of secrecy over most of its activities, is no different. There is no evidence that the ammunition described below is in service with the Regiment. However, it will give the reader some idea of the different types of bullets which are currently available to the counter-terrorist unit. All makes are available in 9mm calibre, as used by the SAS for its hostage-rescue work.

Hydra-Shok bullets are an American invention which are made up into complete rounds by several different manufacturers. The bullet is almost pure lead and, in order to obtain the desired expansion, has a hemispherical recess in the nose which is cast with an upstanding peg in its centre. The head mushrooms on impact and delivers a severe blow, leading to hydraulic compression of body fluid and the transmission of a destructive shock wave – hydrostatic shock. Early Hydra-Shok bullets were found to give irregular deformation, poor accuracy and excessive lead fouling in the weapon. However, these problems now appear to have been dealt with.

The Glaser Safety Slug is another American idea which has found favour among several police forces. The bullet consists of a thin bullet jacket which is filled with compressed bird-shot. Against inanimate objects such as glass and light metal it does not break up, the round having considerable penetrative powers. However, on impact with skin tissue it immediately fragments, releasing the core particles in a cone-shaped pattern of over 330 sub-projectiles. It therefore dumps all its energy into the target and gives good stopping power. Importantly, there is no danger of shoot-through and it cannot ricochet. If the bullet strikes anything at an angle it will simply disintegrate.

The KTW bullet was developed some years ago and has built up an infamous reputation. It has a distinctive green Teflon coating and is simply a lump of cartridge brass. The bullet got the reputation of being a 'cop-killer' because it could go through body armour. However, any solid brass bullet will go through soft armour if it has enough velocity, and the body armour of the 1960s was not as efficient as today's armour.

Far more fearsome is the French Arcane ammunition. The bullet is made of solid copper, is cone-pointed, and has a special propellant charge which gives it high velocity with low chamber pressures, allowing it to be fired from short-barrelled revolvers and pistols. This round really will go through body armour, engine blocks, windscreens, walls and anything else that gets in its way! In addition, after going through these obstacles the bullet does not deform and is still capable of wounding. One drawback to this round is that against soft targets such as flesh it will cause severe wound cavities but will almost certainly pass through the body.

Société Française de Munitions of France produce the THV (*Très Haute Vélocité*) round, a truly ferocious bullet. Looking like a number of traffic bollards stacked one on top of the other, the special shape, coupled with its high velocity, gives it excellent penetrative capabilities. Its effects when it hits the body can be likened to that of a swimmer conducting a belly flop. There is a greatly reduced threat of shoot-through with the THV. For example, fired against Plasticine it produces an 84mm entry hole and stops within 140mm.

One of the drawbacks with hollow point bullets is that they easily misfeed in automatic handguns. Since many European hostage-rescue units, including the SAS, use these for their operations, a way had to be found to remedy this. The German firm Dynamit-Nobel brought out the 9mm Action Safety Bullet 10 years ago.

Above: Lexfoam is explosive liquid foam. It resembles shaving cream and allows a team to blow in doors and windows quickly and effectively. Left: The Browning High Power handgun is carried by all SAS troopers during a hostage-rescue operation. It is a very reliable backup weapon.

This is a fairly standard pistol bullet but has a central hole running through it and a recessed hole in the nose. This is then filled with a plastic peg which is shaped so that the result is a conventionally shaped bullet. On firing, the propellant pressure blows the peg out of the bullet and, because the peg is very light, it is blown clear of the bore before the bullet reaches the muzzle. Therefore what is loaded into the chamber is a conventional round-nose bullet; what comes out of the muzzle is a hollow point round with excellent stopping power and which delivers all its energy on striking.

Two British firms that produce specialist ammunition are the Cobra Gun Company and Conjay Firearms & Ammunition Ltd. The former makes the extremely interesting High Safety Ammunition (HSA). The bullet is an open nosed jacket filled with flechettes. In flight the flechettes remain within the bullet jacket. On striking the target the bullet case will deform and/or split, releasing the flechettes which begin to tumble when hitting flesh, resulting in a very rapid transfer of energy. No shoot-through combines with high tissue damage. Conjay makes the CBX and CBXX Low Penetration rounds which are specifically designed for use in hostage-rescue situations. When hitting the target they do not break up but they do transfer between 65 and 100 per cent of their energy on striking. They are also cause large cavity wounds and massive trauma, thus preventing a terrorist from using a 'last resort' grenade.

TARGET IDENTIFICATION AIDS

Assault teams will often have to enter rooms and buildings that are dark, filled with smoke and/or on fire to rescue hostages. Having the best weapons and ammunition in the world will be to no avail unless they have the means to acquire targets quickly and accurately. Therefore a number of aiming devices have been designed to aid rapid target identification. Aside from infrared and image intensifying sights which, because of their size, are largely employed by snipers (see Chapter 1), there are a number of laser aiming and illuminating devices available to modern hostage-rescue units.

At the Iranian Embassy in 1980, several SAS soldiers had standard torches mounted on their MP5 submachine guns. Though they were rather large and bulky, they were simple to use and were reliable. However, modern systems are much more compact. Laser Products of the US makes the Sure-Fire Tactical Lights range of mounted lights. They are small, powerful light units mounted underneath the weapon's barrel. More powerful than conventional torches, they can be used on shotguns, handguns, submachine guns and rifles.

Another favourite aid is the red aiming dot system which puts a red dot onto the target at the point where the bullet will strike, though

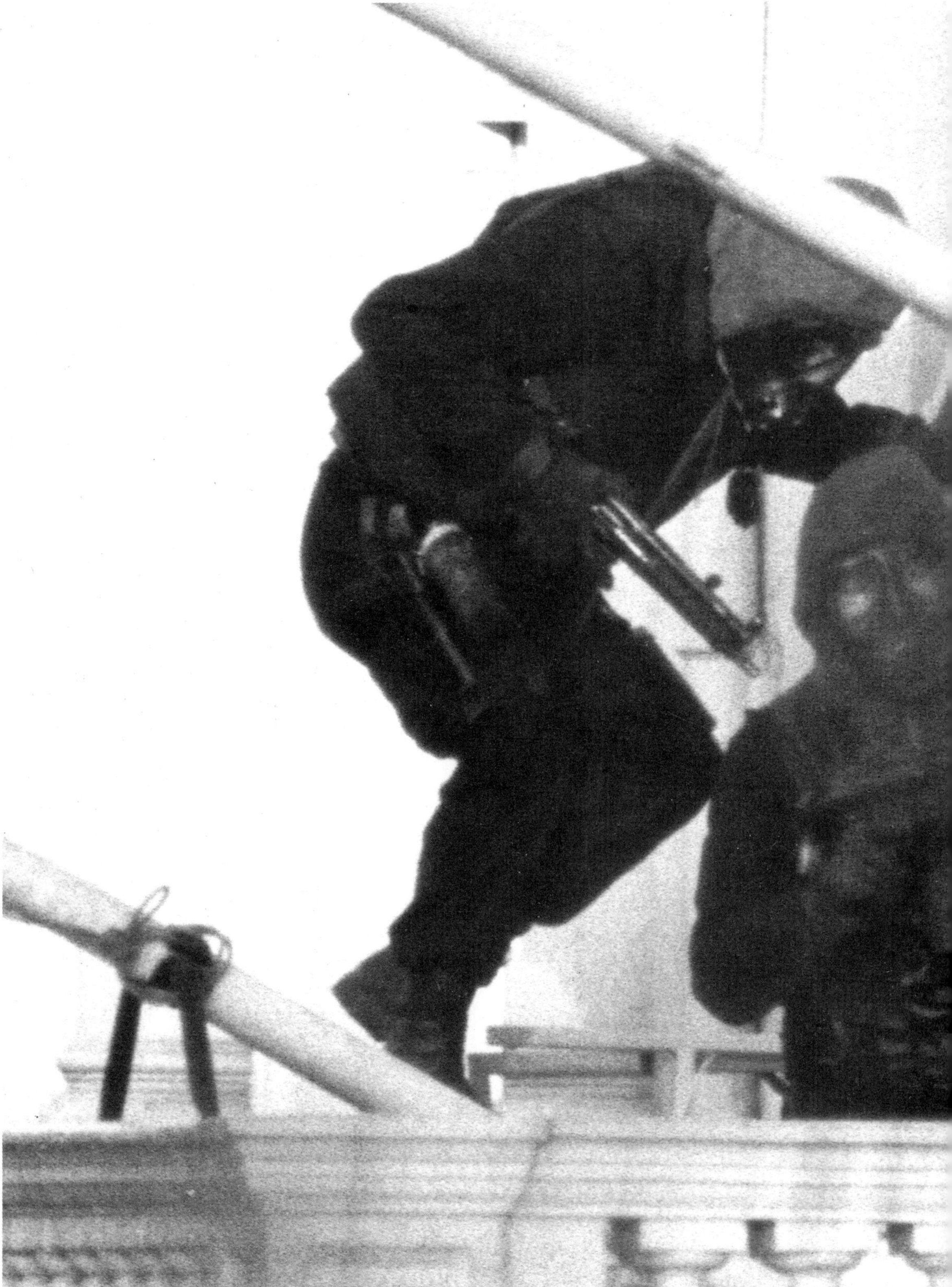

they do not illuminate the target, merely mark it. Nevertheless, these systems greatly aid accurate firing from the hip. Law Enforcement International's LEI-100 laser sight is one of the most powerful red dot laser sights currently available and can be mounted on a number of weapons including the MP5. The sight has a range of 600m and, though it is large, its aluminium construction means it is lightweight. Electro Prismatic Collimators, a UK firm, produces a rather more compact range of red dot aiming devices. They can be fitted to almost any weapon because their small size and light weight means they have a small profile (having a side profile envelope identical to a .357-inch magnum cartridge), enabling the eye to see the foresight and much of the barrel over the top of the sight.

COMMUNICATIONS

Good communications are an essential part of any counter-terrorist work, be it hostage-rescue operations or surveillance and ambush tasks carried out by the SAS in Northern Ireland. Close liaison between assault members during a rescue with snipers and police surrounding the building, or between SAS men and RUC policemen and British Army soldiers in Ulster, can mean the difference between success and bloody failure.

Units such as the SAS look for four main attributes in the communications systems they employ: reliability, compactness, the ability to operate in a hands-off fashion, and the system to be secure. Usually UHF bands are used (see Chapter 4) because they are the most secure. The SAS use the Davies Communications CT100 communications harness for its hostage-rescue work. This comprises the CT100E electronic ear defender headset with earphone for the team radio and socket for connection to the body-worn microphone CT100L. The ear defender allows normal speech to pass at all times, it being possible to electronically restrict high-pressure sound from grenades and gunfire. A second earphone into the earshell allows reception at all times from the assault team

Left: The front of the Iranian Embassy, 5 May 1980. Two SAS soldiers storm the building armed with MP5 submachine guns.

radio. The CT100L body-worn microphone has a large front-mounted press-to-talk button which can be operated by either hand. When it is connected to the SF10 Respirator the body-worn microphone is disabled. Both the body-worn and respirator microphones are operated by depressing a switch on the body or a secondary one worn on the wrist or weapon.

Davies Industrial Communications Ltd of the UK make a number of covert communications devices that are ideally suited for special forces use. These include the M135b covert microphone which can be attached to a standard safety pin and the covert ear worn receiver. Items such as these were worn during the SAS operation against the three IRA terrorists at Gibraltar in March 1988. During that mission, codenamed 'Flavius', the plain clothes SAS soldiers were equipped with radios. One of each pair was tuned into the military command network and the other to the surveillance network. Microphones were positioned in the collars of the men's shirts or jackets, with on/off switches taped to their wrists.

Surprising as it may seem, hand and arm signals are a very useful means of communicating when approaching, searching and clearing an objective. They eliminate unnecessary talking and enhance overall noise discipline. At Princes Gate, for example, two SAS soldiers at the front of the building placed the big 'frame charge' against the window. After it had been placed one of the soldiers gave a hand signal to his comrades below, moments before detonating the charge.

Hand-held transceivers are useful for stakeout and ambush operations conducted in Northern Ireland where individual soldiers may not be within sight of each other and will want to maintain contact with any police or military backup. All special forces transceivers must be compact, lightweight, rugged, easily operated, and have a hands-off operational capability to allow the user to employ his weapon or throw grenades should the need arise. They should also operate in the VHF/UHF frequency range (see Chapter 4) and have built-in encryption

facilities. In addition, for surveillance and plain clothes work they must have covert earpieces and microphones. There are many models currently available, one example being the Landmaster III range of hand-held transceivers built by Pace Communications Ltd of the UK which incorporate encoders, microphones, earphones and which are available in the VHF and UHF frequency ranges. The Covert surveillance communications harness (SKH) made by the British firm Hagen Morfax comprises a webbing harness, miniature microphone and earphone and is ideal for covert operations.

The PVS5400 hand-held radio weighs only 800g and can store 16 preset channels. American systems include Magnavox's AN/PRC-68B transmitter/receiver which can operate in either the VHF band or the FM band. The system, including the battery, weighs only 1.6kg.

**Left: The CT100 communications rig allows team members to talk to each other during a rescue.
Right: Radio Systems Inc's walkie-talkie.**

SURVEILLANCE

In wartime, the SAS is essentially an intelligence-gathering unit that specialises in setting up covert observation posts behind enemy lines. As such, it must have access to sophisticated surveillance equipment to monitor events night and day, and in poor weather conditions.

In early May 1982, a four-man team from G Squadron, 22 SAS, was landed on East Falkland to establish an observation post (OP) near Stanley to watch Argentinian movements and to send intelligence back to the British carrier *Hermes*. The unit was commanded by Captain Aldwin Wight, who would later be awarded a Military Medal for his efforts. The 'hide' he and his men established had a turf roof that blended into the surrounding terrain. Inside the OP conditions were cramped and damp: there was no source of natural light, only a small hole to allow a powerful telescope to be pointed in the direction of Stanley. During the day there was no opportunity for the men to stretch their limbs or to eat any warm food. Cheese, biscuits and chocolate were eaten during the day, with warm soup taken at night. Only under the cover of darkness could the men leave the OP and stretch, their limbs numb from constricted circulation.

Despite the conditions, Wight and his team maintained the OP undetected for a total of 26 days, continually sending

A Royal Marines observation post (OP) in Norway. OPs usually contain a wide variety of viewing, listening and communications equipment, in addition to the men's supplies.

radio signals concerning enemy activity around Stanley, probably using 'burst' transmissions (see Chapter 4) to defeat Argentine direction-finding equipment.

Despite the image of the SAS as being black-clad anti-terrorist soldiers, the Regiment's true wartime role is one of intelligence gathering. Using their high levels of fieldcraft, four-man SAS teams can infiltrate deep behind enemy lines and establish OPs. From these they can provide a constant flow of accurate intelligence about troop and equipment movements, locations of headquarters, airfields and so on. In such a role the SAS can achieve results out of all proportion to its size, and can be a war-winning unit. The work requires courage and patience; but it also needs the right kind of equipment.

The intelligence-gathering role is perhaps seen at its clearest in Northern Ireland. This can be just as dangerous as setting up OPs in the Falklands, especially in such areas as South Armagh – 'bandit country'. There are no columns of tanks or soldiers to be counted, no headquarters or generals to be identified, but the task is just as demanding as in more conventional warfare. The operatives of the IRA, far from being the reckless, trigger-happy urban fighters of the early 1970s, are now skilled, often highly trained, men and women who are well aware that the security forces are observing them. And the SAS soldiers tasked with watching potential terrorists must have access to sophisticated devices: image intensifying, infrared and thermal imaging equipment – hardware that can enable suspects to be watched and photographed day and night, and in all weather conditions.

This chapter gives examples of the current types of surveillance and intelligence-gathering equipment available to specialist units such as the SAS. As with many things concerning the latter, there is no certain way of knowing what surveillance equipment is used by the Regiment, though the examples discussed below all have attributes that make them suitable for special forces work.

INFRARED

Infrared (IR) radiation (infrared is between 1.5 and 14 microns on the electromagnetic spectrum) is emitted by all objects warmer than absolute zero (-273 degrees Centigrade). The hotter an object is, the greater the magnitude of IR energy it emits.

There are three broad bands of the IR spectrum: near- or short-wavelength infrared (SWIR) – 1.5 to 4.5 microns; mid-wavelength infrared (MWIR) – 4.5 to eight microns; and far- or long-wavelength infrared (LWIR) – eight to 14 microns. As a rule, the hotter the object the shorter the wavelength of its IR emissions.

For military purposes the IR spectrum is reduced to two frequencies or 'windows': between two and three microns and between eight and 14 microns. For ground surveillance purposes the SWIR frequency is used, being able to detect objects with temperatures greater than 80 degrees Fahrenheit (vehicles, aircraft, ships and troops).

How do IR sensors work? They optically focus IR radiation on a focal plane of photo-electric detectors that are tuned to specific wavelengths. The simplest detectors are of the lead sulphide type. They are easy to make but are relatively insensitive. Advanced sensors are cryogenically cooled by a gas bottle or cryomotor to suppress the 'noise' generated by the heat of their own optics and electronics.

IR surveillance devices fall into two categories: semi-active and passive. The former require an infrared light to illuminate objects in their field of view. Passive IR devices, also known as thermal imagers, need no illumination and convert infrared emissions into video images. Modern sights are not particularly heavy or bulky, but they can be delicate. In addition, they require constant cooling, making them unsuitable for general field use with specialist units such as the SAS.

THERMAL IMAGING

In thermal imaging devices, IR radiation from objects is focused by optics onto a focal plane array of IR detectors. They are then converted into video images by electronic signal processing. Thermal imaging devices are able to operate in the total absence of light and can also penetrate smoke and fog.

Above right: A modern hand-held thermal imager.
Below right: Thorn EMI's multi-role thermal imager.

IMAGE INTENSIFIERS

These are night vision devices that operate by amplifying low levels of visible light by up to 100,000 times to create a daylight image. The light, however minute, is collected by a lens and focused on a photo-cathode. The latter in turn releases electrons when it absorbs photons of light. The electrons are then accelerated by an electrical field and projected onto a screen to generate a bright image.

There are two methods to improve image intensification. First, several image intensifier tubes can be coupled in a series called a 'cascade' array. However, the resolution is poor because of the distortion of the original image as it passes through each stage of amplification. The second method is channel electron amplification: this relies on tubes lined with semi-conductor glass, formed into fibrescopic mosaics and inserted between a photo-cathode and a screen. As the electrons generated by the photo-cathode collide

Above: Davin's Modulux image intensifier is ideal for surveillance in low light. It can be fitted to most 35mm SLR cameras.

with the semi-conductor tubes, additional electrons are released which are accelerated by an electrical field and projected onto the screen. Channel tubes are lighter and smaller than 'cascade' arrays and have a higher resolution.

Image intensifiers are used as night sights, for surveillance and as individual night vision goggles (the latter can be rather bulky and uncomfortable to wear). However, their effectiveness is reduced by smoke, fog, dense foliage and heavy precipitation because they work only in the visible spectrum.

VIEWING EQUIPMENT

Surveillance operations are inevitably mentally and physically draining for the soldiers involved. Spending days, perhaps weeks, in a confined space, trying to spot and to record the movements of suspects, continually worrying about being discovered; these stresses can tax even the most highly trained soldiers. The equipment they use must also withstand the sometimes rough treatment handed out to it, as well as perform its allotted task. There are many different types of viewing devices designed for military surveillance currently available, and most of them are able to work on a 24-hour basis.

The UK firm Davin Optical Ltd produce a number of systems including the Modulux, Minimodulux, Minilux and Spylux models. The latter is an effective night viewer capable of operating in both rural and urban areas at night. The unit incorporates a first generation image intensifier which gives a high resolution, low noise image enabling target acquisition beyond 200m in low light conditions. It has the added advantage of being able to work in urban areas as bright light sources cause the unit only minimal interference. Weighing only 0.85kg and having a battery life of around 90 hours, the Spylux is ideal for covert operations.

Below: Military surveillance equipment is frequently employed in Londonderry, an area of Northern Ireland noted for its Republican activity.

The Maxilux M system has been designed specifically for military users for passive long-range acquisition and recognition down to starlight illumination levels. Incorporating a high-grain image intensifier, the system is manportable, fully sealed and designed for rugged field use. The image intensifier is of the three-stage 'cascade' type and each battery gives the unit up to 50 hours of use. The unit weighs 7.8kg. In addition, the Maxilux P version is a photographic unit available with a low noise, low distortion intensifier tube and with optional fittings for closed circuit television (CCTV), 35mm photography and a binocular viewer lens for long-term visual surveillance.

The Minilux is a night viewer designed for use with 35mm cameras or CCTV systems. Capable of giving a times three magnification, the unit gives very high quality images. The Minimodulux is a small, compact night vision system which can be used as a hand-held night viewer or for photography and filming at night. Incorporating an image intensifying tube, the unit has full flash protection, automatic brightness control and bright light suppression for use in both rural and urban environments. Weighing only 1.6kg, the unit is in service with the British Army and UK police forces.

The Modulux night vision system is perhaps one of the most effective in Davin's range. Incorporating a high resolution, low distortion image intensifying tube which amplifies light by a factor of times 250,000, the system is compatible with all commercially available cameras and lenses. It can operate in any one of three modes. First, for photography the Modulux can be fitted to any 35mm camera, with the camera viewfinder being used for observation. Second, for observation the system can be fitted with either a biocular or monocular lens for night-time work. Third, the Modulux can be fitted to any standard CCTV camera, the scene being viewed on a remote monitor or recorded with a video cassette recorder.

There are a number of thermal imaging systems currently available, all designed for use on the battlefield and so ideally suited to SAS-type operations. Hawkeye Systems of the UK, for example, produce the Model HT10 thermal imaging camera. It is lightweight and compact, and incorporates a silent internal closed-cycle cooler which can be operated from its own replaceable battery and requires no cooling gas or logistic support. It is capable of detecting men, vehicles and aircraft at long ranges and in low light conditions or in no light at all. Even when the target is obscured by dust or haze, it is capable of producing a high quality video picture. The thermal picture is displayed on an integral video monitor for direct viewing or can be displayed on a separate monitor for remote

Below: The Minimodulux hand-held image intensifer can be used as a night vision scope or for photography and filming at night. It is currently in service with the British Army.

applications. The optical system is capable of a times seven magnification. A feature that is useful for OP work is the remote display facility.

Thorn EMI Electronics Ltd make the hand-held thermal imager, a compact observation device that can be mounted on a tripod with a laser rangefinder to direct fire or form part of a weapon aiming system. Capable of being carried round the neck, the unit weighs 5kg.

Ever since World War II SAS soldiers have carried cameras with them on their operations to record their exploits. Tony Geraghty's book, *This is the SAS*, is testimony to this, being a pictorial history of the Regiment. However, photographs were not only useful as reminders to individuals of a particular action or campaign. They were also invaluable to the intelligence agencies who were trying to build up an overall picture of enemy intentions and strengths. They were particularly keen to get hold of SAS shots as the latter's men were invariably operating behind enemy lines, or at least on the frontline, and any intelligence they provided could be crucial. Thus in Borneo, SAS troopers would take pictures of dead enemy personnel before retreating after an ambush or contact. These would then be forwarded to the Intelligence Corps for subsequent dissemination and analysis.

Currently there are many cameras available, all offering state-of-the-art technology and a mind-boggling number of facilities. However, SAS teams on extended operations will be looking for reliability and ruggedness from their cameras. The Japanese firm Nikon produces a wide range of 35mm cameras including the top of the range F-801. This model includes a Matrix Metering system for correct exposure in difficult lighting situations, an advanced autofocus, electronic rangefinder and long exposure. Nikon's F3HP has a titanium body (which means the camera can take a lot of punishment), while the whole camera weighs only 760g.

CCTV has become an increasingly important part of the war against terrorism, both in Northern Ireland and during hostage-rescue operations. P.W. Allen & Co of the UK make the RS 445 fibre optic surveillance set which is specifically designed for covert surveillance work. It has a fibre optic lens which means it can

be positioned away from the observer if need be. Therefore, the camera need not be located in the SAS soldier's hide. Tanny Ltd, another UK firm, offer a range of high quality CCTV cameras suitable for OP work. They are robust, lightweight units which are easy to install. In addition, they can be used in varying light conditions ranging from daylight down to starlight.

AUDIO AND LASER SYSTEMS

The US firm Surveillance Technology Group produce a number of systems designed for covert surveillance work. For covert observation and surveillance work in Northern Ireland they would be ideal for units such as the SAS. The audio surveillance probe allows conversations to be monitored through normally inaccessible walls or partitions. The unit consists of a lens and high grain microphone probe which is only 8mm in diameter. The probe can be coupled to any combination of optional tape recorder, 35mm camera or CCTV system.

The firm's laser surveillance system can be used from outside the premises under surveillance. Normal conversations within a room create minute vibrations on exterior windows which act much like a diaphragm of a microphone oscillating with sound waves. Within a line-of-sight path, the system's tripod-mounted transmitter directs an invisible beam onto the window, collecting modulated vibrations. The beam then bounces back to an optical receiver which converts the modulated beam into audio signals. The latter are then filtered, amplified and converted into clear conversations. The resulting conversation can be monitored through headphones and simultaneously recorded for later examination. For stable monitoring both the transmitter and optical receiver are tripod-mounted.

LASER DESIGNATORS

During late August 1990, elements of 22 SAS were flown into Saudi Arabia as part of Operation 'Desert Shield', the UN military buildup to prevent further Iraqi military expansion in the Persian Gulf following Saddam Hussein's invasion of Kuwait . The men were reportedly carrying large quantities of laser

Above: Military binoculars are simple pieces of kit which are essential for surveying terrain.
Left: SAS soldiers have, since World War II, always carried cameras with them when on operations. Photographs taken behind enemy lines can be a great asset to military intelligence.

designators to help Allied aircraft deliver their bombs accurately onto targets in Kuwait and Iraq. During the air campaign that was to be the first stage of the liberation of Kuwait, US and British special forces played a vital part in directing bombs onto their targets.

The first phase of the war, which began with Allied aircraft launching attacks on 16 January 1991, was directed against the Iraqi Air Force, ground-based air defence system, communications systems, nuclear, biological and chemical research facilities, and all military production centres. On the ground special forces units, inserted before the air campaign began, designated targets for airborne laser guided bombs with their laser designators.

The laser designator is a device that 'illuminates' the target with a laser beam so it

can be detected by the seekers inside laser guided bombs. In the Gulf, the SAS used hand-held laser designators, which can also be mounted on ships, aircraft and ground vehicles if required. The devices also incorporate a laser rangefinder which calculates the distance from the designator to the target by the delay between the transmission of the beam and the reception of laser radiation reflected back from the target. Laser guided bombs used in the Gulf included the GBU-15 electro-optically guided bomb and the GBU-10 Paveway II. In these weapons the seeker head contains a silicon detector array divided into quadrants. The laser radiation received by the detector is then converted into electrical impulses which allow the guidance computer to steer the bomb towards its target. The target must be illuminated by the designator throughout the whole of its flight. Though the aircraft dropping a bomb can act as a designator, it is much better, to enable it to leave the area as quickly as possible to avoid anti-aircraft fire, if the laser designator is operated from a ground position (in this way it can also illuminate targets for several aircraft).

CLOTHING

The soldiers of the Special Air Service must have the proper clothing to enable them to fight in any terrain in the world, from the deserts of the Middle East to the freezing wastes of the arctic.

One of the less glamorous, though vitally important, aspects of preparing for any military campaign or operation is the selection of the clothing best suited to the work in hand. Without proper attention to clothing the mission can suffer, or even fail, and so the SAS, like other military units, ensures its men are properly clothed.

This chapter will not attempt to list every piece of clothing the Regiment's soldiers have worn since 1941; rather, it will describe the main types of dress currently worn by SAS troops in different types of terrain.

There are basically three main dangers the special forces soldier faces on active duty: the threat posed by the enemy, diseases and injuries, and environmental threats. The latter is subdivided into 'thermal insults', i.e. extremes of temperature, and 'nutritional insults' (lack of food and/or water or toxic food and/or water). The SAS soldier is taught he has three containers in which he can carry equipment to defend himself against these threats. First, his person; things can be carried in the seams and pockets of smocks (though not trouser pockets because this inhibits movement). Second, the belt kit is a useful carrying tool (braces are essential as they allow the belt to hang on the shoulders if the weather is hot, rather than being drawn tight around the waist). The third container is the bergen which can carry large loads.

A soldier wearing Disruptive Pattern Material (DPM) clothing. Such dress is standard-issue for British soldiers operating in temperate weather conditions.

Section I
DESERT CLOTHING

Footwear SAS soldiers have generally worn two types of footwear for desert campaigns – though during the Omani campaign in the 1970s individual troopers often purchased their own from high street shops. The first is the ankle-length desert boot – comfortable but with a tendency to split at the seams. Second, and currently used by the Regiment, is the high-neck desert boot. Socks are never worn in the desert because they produce sweat and rot very quickly. SAS soldiers have, however, been known to wrap masking tape around their feet before they put on their boots.

Desert and arid conditions affect boots badly, as 'Lofty' Large relates of the 1959 SAS campaign in northern Oman: 'Our boots, which had rubber soles, were worn down so that the screws which had held the soles on were like football boot studs with rubber washers under them. The toe caps were mostly worn away and some of us had our toes showing through. After six weeks a re-supply of boots was most welcome.'

Sandals are never worn by troops in the desert. This may, at first, seem rather surprising because they are, after all, loose and they allow the feet to breathe. They leave the top of the foot exposed to the sun which can cause sunburn, however, and they expose feet to insects that bite or, much more serious, burrow into the toes and lay eggs.

Trousers The main type of trousers worn in the desert are the lightweight cotton, desert Disruptive Pattern Material (DPM) variety (nylon is never worn as it is too hot). They are very loose and give the wearer good protection against the sun. Pictures of the SAS in Oman during the 1970s often featured SAS soldiers wearing shorts. Though lightweight tropical shorts are sometimes worn when men are on stand-down, they are generally not worn on active duty for two reasons. First, the legs are exposed to the sun which can cause sunburn (the aforementioned SAS troopers in Oman had been in the country for many months and had

therefore acclimatised to the local conditions). Second, uncovered bodies lose a lot of sweat through evaporation and therefore requires a soldier to drink water to replace the lost fluid. A loose covering of clothing means there is a layer of insulating air and any sweat will cool the wearer more efficiently. And it can get very cold at night in the desert – trousers keep the wearer much warmer than shorts.

Shirts In the desert, cotton DPM, long-sleeved shirts are worn. Like trousers they are very loose and baggy and are coloured brown and yellow. Long sleeves prevent the arms being exposed to the sun.

For night wear troopers have been known to take the desert woolly pully and the 'fitzroy' jacket. The latter is made from green nylon with hollow-fill and fits into a stuff sack at the bottom of a bergen.

Troopers wear a variety of gloves in the desert, including US Army pilot's gloves made from green Nomex and ordinary mittens with the fingers cut off. An additional layer of protection that is frequently used is the SAS smock. Being very baggy it is ideal for desert conditions.

Headgear To prevent sunstroke and sunburn, all SAS troopers, and soldiers in general, wear some sort of headgear in the desert. The best is probably the native *shemagh* which is often dyed yellow. It traps cool air underneath, protects the wearer's neck and is also large enough to be turned into an improvised shelter if need be.

Generally sunglasses are not worn by SAS soldiers on operations. Tinted goggles are preferred because they are more secure than sunglasses and, more importantly, when a patrol is moving through the desert on vehicles, goggles will provide the soldiers with more protection against the clouds of dust and sand thrown up by the transport's wheels.

**Above right: This SAS soldier in Oman is well protected from the ravages of the sun.
Below right. Modern British Army desert clothing.**

Section 2
ARCTIC CLOTHING

Arctic regions are characterised by snow and ice and extremes of cold and harsh winds. The latter two combined produce what is called windchill. For example, if the temperature is minus 20 degrees Fahrenheit and there is a wind of 20 knots, the equivalent chill factor is minus 75 degrees Fahrenheit! Under these conditions exposed flesh can freeze within 30 seconds. The clothing worn by soldiers must, therefore, offer protection against the wind and cold. The secret of cold weather clothing is layers as opposed to weight. Loose-fitting clothes worn in layers allow the blood to circulate freely and help prevent frostbite (the freezing of parts of the body when exposed to temperatures below freezing; skin initially turns red and then pale grey or white).

In arctic conditions the whole body must be protected, as well as hands and feet. Generally speaking, the key to survival in these areas is to keep all clothing clean (dirt and grease clog air spaces and therefore reduce ventilation), avoid overheating (the body sweats to keep cool when it is hot, and in the arctic sweat can freeze very quickly – in cold weather it is always better being a little cool rather than running the risk of sweating), wear clothing loose to allow air to circulate, and try to keep clothing dry on both the inside and outside.

Underwear In very cold conditions cotton long johns are worn by soldiers underneath their clothing. These dark green items of clothing, worn next to the skin, are tight up to the knee, but from the knee to the groin are baggy to trap air for heat insulation. The upper vest is long-sleeved but has elasticated wrists to prevent the escape of heat.

Footwear Keeping feet warm and dry in arctic conditions can be very difficult. Therefore troopers usually wear two pairs of good quality mountaineering socks over the feet – a wool pair next to the skin and a nylon pair on top (wool does not absorb water and stays warm even when damp; cotton, on the other hand, absorbs

moisture and loses heat very quickly when wet). Feet always sweat when active and, because the boots are waterproof, the moisture will remain inside the socks or in the bottom of the boots. However, the feet remain warm because the heat given off by the body remains inside the boots.

Gore-tex seals are worn over the socks. Gore-tex is a 'breathable' material which allows perspiration vapour to exit but prevents water from entering. This is achieved because of the microporous Gore-Tex membrane which has nine billion pores per square inch. These pores are 20,000 times smaller than a droplet of water but 700 times larger than a molecule of water vapour. This prevents the entry of wind and water but allows perspiration to escape freely.

The boots – such as Berghaus mountain boots – are then put on. Berghaus are particularly good because they have a cleat which enables the wearer to put on Gore-tex gaiters if required. Boots must also be able to clip onto skis (with the British Army arctic ski the boot is held front and back, however SAS soldiers tend to have their own, often expensive, private skis which are clipped on at the toes only, and they also apply the best commercial wax to them). Snow shoes are also used in polar regions. Though skis are much faster, skiing in deep, loose snow, for example, is exhausting and snow shoes will therefore be employed.

Trousers SAS soldiers usually wear Royal Marine cotton DPM trousers in polar regions because they have a velcro slash from the ankle to the knee to allow a quick change to be made if necessary. They also have velcro pockets and large buttons (all arctic clothing has large buttons because the soldiers are invariably wearing gloves).

Shirt In polar regions no shirt is worn; rather, a Gore-tex smock would be worn (SAS smocks are

Above right: Royal Marines with arctic kit. Note face masks, essential for defence against the cold. Below right: Note the white bergen covers.

equipped with hoods). When a patrol is moving slowly or has stopped, a 'fitzroy' would be put on beneath the smock. In addition, troops would also wear a light, white nylon trouser, smock and bergen cover. The use of gloves is essential in polar regions to prevent the loss of fingers from frostbite. SAS soldiers have traditionally worn Northern Ireland-issue gloves or commercial ski gloves, though with the latter the thickness of the fingers presents problems when firing a weapon. Alternatively, two pairs of gloves can be worn, an inner pair of thin cotton and an outer pair of white nylon. Mittens can be worn over a pair of gloves, though for firing purposes the right one has to be immediately removed (some soldiers attach tape from the torso to the mitten which allows the mitten to be yanked off quickly if necessary).

Headgear Woolly hats are favoured by the Regiment, though balaclavas are also worn. The problem with the latter is that they inhibit hearing – and sometimes the enemy can be heard before he is seen. In addition, face masks are worn. These consist of a thin silk lining which goes next to the skin and an outer lining of cotton. They are popular at night, when the temperature drops severely.

Goggles are usually worn in polar regions to prevent snow blindness (caused by the ultraviolet rays of the sun reflecting from a snow-covered surface). The goggles are the same as those worn in the desert, with the addition of white tape for camouflage purposes. Failure to wear them can prove painful: the eyes feel gritty, they become red, they water, and eventually the sufferer will get a headache (the treatment includes blindfolding the victim temporarily).

Surprising as it may seem, soldiers can get sunburned in cold climates more easily than in warm regions because the rays of the sun reflect upwards from the snow and ice. Vulnerable areas include the lips, eyelids and around and up the nose. Therefore, soldiers often apply sunburn cream or chapstick to these areas, as well as up the nose.

Right: To prevent frostbite in the arctic it is essential to protect the skin. Thus this soldier is equipped with mittens and a face mask.

JUNGLE CLOTHING

Tropical regions are characterised by dense jungle, heavy rainfall, severe humidity and high temperatures. In these conditions it might seem best for a soldier to wear as little as possible (as the natives do). Unfortunately, as in the desert, troops need to cover up to prevent being scratched, bitten and stung. Everyone invariably sweats a great deal in tropical regions and so clothes quickly become saturated (it is almost impossible to keep them dry). Eventually they will rot, especially footwear and underwear. During the Malayan campaign, for example, British officers, including SAS, often had their own clothes made by local tailors. Called 'pea greens', the material was fine but it was discovered that the thread was the Achilles heel. Men sweated into it, it hardened and then immediately fell apart.

Footwear Good footwear is essential for tropical areas. When walking through the jungle most creatures – snakes, wild pigs and large mammals – will move away, but there is still a risk of walking into a scorpion or spider's nest. In addition, leeches and centipedes are an ever-present menace. Any bite or sting can quickly turn into an infection or disease, and germs breed at an alarming rate in the jungle.

It is usual for soldiers to apply powder on their feet as defence against athlete's foot, though regular washing and airing of the feet is also very important.

The type of boot worn in tropical conditions by troopers is the rubber and canvas variety. American soldiers on jungle patrols during the Vietnam War sometimes stood on pungi stakes (sharpened bamboo stakes that had excrement smeared on the pointed end) which pierced the rubber sole and inflicted a nasty, though rarely fatal, wound. A way round this was to fit military boots with what was called a 'riveter's cleat', a metal plate inserted in the sole which prevented sharp objects going through the sole and into the foot. SAS soldiers also wear this type of boot, the uppers being leather and the rest canvas.

Trousers Shorts are never worn in the jungle because of the threats posed by bites and scratches. SAS soldiers usually wear trousers that are loose, baggy and which have a drawcord waist, cross-overs and button flies. The Americans believe that a man should go into the jungle 'lean and mean' to fight. The problem with this is that when he comes out he may be even leaner and will resemble a walking skeleton. The British take a different approach. They encourage soldiers, especially those who will be in the jungle for a long time on extended operations, to bulk up and go in fat. In the jungle they will lose a lot of weight. Hence the need for adjustable waist bands.

Shirt Like trousers, shirts worn in the tropics are of the cotton DPM, olive-green variety, and they are long-sleeved to provide protection against bites and scratches.

Headgear In the jungle most troopers wear the jungle hat, known as the hat, DPM, tropical. Most SAS troops carry nylon cord with them on operations which they attach to items such as hats and then tie them to their smocks and shirts. There is a very good reason for this: if a patrol has to run like hell then hats and other bits of kit will not be left behind but will stay attached to the body.

Bandanas In the jungle SAS troops will often wear olive-green veils as sweatbands around their heads to keep sweat out of their eyes. They may also be worn around the neck – as in Borneo in the 1960s.

Above right: An SAS trooper in Borneo in the 1960s. Note his bergen, M16 rifle and his sweat-covered clothes. Because of the high humidity it is impossible to keep dry in the jungle. Despite the heat, the trooper keeps his arms and head covered for protection against bites, scratches and stings. Below right: Grenadier Guardsmen in Brunei. Their jungle kit includes machetes, which are also used by SAS soldiers in jungle terrain.

Section 4
TEMPERATE CLOTHING

'Towards the end of the first afternoon, a heavy squall hit us. It was vicious in its suddenness and its intensity. We were caught without our windproofs, our shirts unbuttoned to the waist. Within seconds my hair was matted against my forehead and rivulets of water ran down my neck and over my chest. I was quickly soaked through, my OGs clinging clammily to my skin.' (Soldier 'I' in the Black Mountains)

Temperate weather conditions can present a dilemma to soldiers because they are mostly somewhere in between being too hot or too cold. Inevitably, temperate areas are characterised by intermittent wind and rain, with the latter being the drizzle variety that soaks everything and makes for a thoroughly miserable time. The type of clothing worn by soldiers therefore reflects these conditions.

Footwear Most SAS troopers wear the standard-issue British Army boots, though some have been known to purchase their own, such as Danner boots which are made out of full grain leather and cordura nylon and have a Gore-tex lining. The latter are substantially better than the standard-issue variety, though they have received criticism concerning their lack of support around the ankle.

Trousers The SAS wear the standard DPM windproof tight-weave cotton variety (in Northern Ireland, for example, troopers will endeavour to look as much like ordinary soldiers as possible so as not to arouse too much suspicion).

Smocks SAS soldiers will usually wear the standard-issue combat smock which is big, loose and baggy. Occasionally, they will also wear a Helly-Hansen cold weather pullover which has a velcro closure at the neck.

Headgear SAS soldiers usually wear some form of headgear, though very rarely helmets (they endeavour to be in positions where they will not require hard headgear, i.e. well away from where

artillery or mortar rounds are falling). The peaked camouflaged combat cap is favoured. As a general rule, beige berets sporting the Winged Dagger SAS badge are rarely worn on active duty. The Regiment likes to keep a low profile as far as its activities are concerned and thus frowns upon individual soldiers drawing unnecessary attention to themselves. This secrecy is a consequence of the SAS's role in Northern Ireland and its assumption of general counter-terrorist responsibilities.

Civilian clothes SAS soldiers frequently undertake plain clothes work as part of their anti-terrorist duties. In addition, the Regiment likes to keep the comings and goings of its men, especially in Ulster, shrouded in secrecy. This entails highly trained and superbly fit soldiers trying to turn themselves into 'average' civilians. Though this may sound comical, in Northern Ireland it is deadly serious as the compromise of a soldier's cover can result in his death.

Soldier 'I' provides an amusing record of his team's arrival at the port of Belfast in the early 1970s: 'Even though we had dressed down in our Oxfam reject specials to give the impression of itinerant building-site workers or casual hotel staff...it was extremely difficult for a team of highly alert men who had spent weeks and months as a family, eating, sleeping, drinking and training together, to melt unobserved and unobserving into the background...a dozen heavies with long hair and second-hand clothes trying desperately to look inconspicuous.'

During the operation against the IRA Active Service Unit at Gibraltar in March 1988, for example, the SAS soldiers were wearing civilian jackets and sports shirts. However, when it came to the actual confrontation with the terrorists, the latter, when eye-to-eye contact was made, knew who they were facing (according to the soldiers at the subsequent inquest). It is difficult to disguise the bearing of an SAS soldier, it seems.

Above right: Two soldiers dressed in olive-greens.
Below right: British Army DPM clothing.

BELTS AND BERGENS

SAS soldiers are renowned for their ability to carry heavy loads on their backs over long distances. The supplies and equipment they carry in their bergens and on their belts allow them to live and fight behind enemy lines.

The physical stamina of SAS soldiers is legend. The rigours of Selection Training are not designed to be just a sadistic exercise in seeing how much a man can take before he drops, far from it. Rather, it is to find out whether prospective recruits can shoulder the sort of loads for long periods they might be called upon to carry when they are on active duty. The following quote from Soldier 'I' concerning the campaign in Oman in the early 1970s is typical of the 'donkey work' undertaken by SAS soldiers in wartime: 'I would have to carry a GPMG tripod, weighing over thirty pounds, plus 1000 rounds of GPMG link ammunition – 500 wrapped around the body and 500 in the bergen. This was before the rations, water, belt kit and personal weapon, a self-loading rifle, were taken into consideration. And all in the heat of an Arabian night.'

Over 10 years before it had been the same for SAS troopers involved involved in the assault on the Jebel Akhdar in the north of Oman. According to Lieutenant-Colonel Johnny Cooper, one of the SAS 'Originals', the strength and stamina of the Regiment's soldiers was the key to success: 'It had to be done quickly. If you'd sent in a battalion of infantry it would have cost a lot of money. Here, you were sending only a small gang. It was an SAS job because we had the ability to carry pack-mule loads and we were all very fit.'

Two British Paras shelter under a basha in bad weather. Though SAS soldiers do use commercial bashas, they are also taught to construct them from locally available materials.

Bergens Bergens are an extremely important, if rather mundane, piece of SAS kit, because a soldier lives out of his bergen – any supplies carried on the belt are usually for emergencies. The SAS prefers the external square-frame bergen, either the 60-litre Cyclops or the 80-litre Crusader, as opposed to the new British Army Personal Load Carrying Equipment (PLCE). However, the problem with bergens – which is experienced by all military personnel the world over – is that the greater their capacity the more a soldier will put into them. Overall this is counter-productive to the survival mentality.

What actually goes inside the bergen? SAS soldiers have a list of priorities concerning what the contents should be. The order of priority is as follows: ammunition, water, food and clothing (bivvy bags are usually carried on the belt). Other things that may be carried include spare radio batteries (in the case of the patrol signaller), a medical pack (if the wearer is the patrol medic), explosives (if the demolitions expert), extra GPMG ammunition, Claymore mines, mortar ammunition, and a laser target designator for aircraft targeting purposes.

Rations are obviously an important part of any patrol's supplies. SAS soldiers usually carry around 14 day's supply of food, though a man can get two day's rations out of a one-day pack if necessary. The aim of modern long-range reconnaissance patrol (LRRP) rations is to provide the individual trooper with high energy. In addition, there has been a move away from tins to plastic containers in an effort to save weight and improve ease of opening. Most food that is carried – rice and stew-like meals – is pre-cooked which saves having to light a hexamine stove in order to eat rations. In addition, each trooper will carry a hot brew pack and high-calorie foods such as candy, chocolate and sweets. Aluminium water bottles are used as opposed to plastic ones because you cannot heat the latter in a fire (extra water is always carried in the bergen).

Belt kits These are an important part of an SAS soldier's equipment and, in an emergency, can save his life. The idea with a belt is to keep the area from hip bone to hip bone at the front clear to aid movement. On the left side of the belt the primary requirement is access to spare magazines because men usually pull the trigger with the fingers of their right hand and change magazines with their left. Therefore magazine pouches will be carried on the left side.

On the right side will be a compass pouch, an escape and evasion pouch, a survival/utility knife (this is similar to a machete in appearance and is good for hacking through wood – its primary purpose is for construction), water bottles (two or three plus a water filter), a pouch for the bivvy bag, a bayonet, then two ammunition pouches on the left-hand side (the SAS use double ammunition pouches, i.e. there are two magazines in each pouch). Some troopers also like to wear a Browning High Power handgun on the right hip.

Medical kits The British Combat Training Team places life support – airways, breathing and circulation – above trauma management - arterial bleeding, broken bones and cover burns – in its list of priorities in the treatment of military casualties. SAS medical kits usually follow these priorities, their contents also being pitched at the level of confidence of the patrol medic, which is usually very high.

What items go into a medical kit? Standard contents would include a paediatric mucus extractor to suck out debris from a gunshot wound; a blood volume expander; infusion fluid (similar to blood); and dressings. The latter would need to be Nuclear, Biological and Chemical (NBC) proof if the patrol was operating in an NBC environment. If this was the case the medic would also be carrying an SF10 respirator. Other medical equipment carried would include artery forceps to clip off arteries which are bleeding; a suture kit; and fracture straps which can double as aircraft marker panels; and burns dressings.

The medic will also be carrying a pharmaceutical pack to fight infections which will consist of antibiotic tablets and antibiotics in injectable form; pre-packed, pre-dosed injections for NBC environments; pain killers (such as morphine derivatives and aspirin); flamazine cream to prevent local infection when treating burns; and creams for dealing with fungal problems around the body's sweaty parts.

Survival kits Worn on the belt by all SAS soldiers, the survival kit is small but contains some extremely useful items: ready-to-eat emergency rations which will sustain a man for two days; vacuum-compressed plastic sheets; a small map of the area he is operating in; a 'button' compass; fishing line and weights; snares (brass picture wire with eyelets and cord); lengths of nylon cord (alternatively, extra-long boot laces can be worn); flint and steel for making fires; a utility knife; chemicals such as potassium permanganate which can be used as a marker in the snow; and some sort of writing implement, probably a pencil.

Other items in the survival kit would probably include curry powder so the trooper can eat almost anything and taste nothing but the powder. Water purification tablets are also usually included. However, the real survival kit is the soldier's own skills in knowing how to live off the land, evade the enemy and get back to friendly territory.

Above: The kit needed for an offensive patrol.
Right: Modern British Army load-carrying kit.

MAIN EQUIPMENT FEATURED